PRESENTED TO:

_____

BY:

_____

DATE:

_____

Print ISBN 978-1-68322-433-4

Published by Barbour Books, an imprint of Barbour Publishing, Inc., 1810 Barbour Drive, Uhrichsville, Ohio 44683, www.barbourbooks.com

Our mission is to inspire the world with the life-changing message of the Bible.

 Member of the
Evangelical Christian
Publishers Association

Printed in the United States of America.

JEAN FISCHER

3-MINUTE
PRAYERS
FOR GRADS

BARBOUR BOOKS
An Imprint of Barbour Publishing, Inc.

INTRODUCTION

Got 3 minutes, grad?

You'll find just the wisdom you need in *3-Minute Prayers for Grads*.

This practical, encouraging book packs a powerful dose of inspiration into 3 short minutes.

* Minute 1: scripture to meditate on

* Minute 2: a just-right-sized devotional prayer

* Minute 3: a question for further reflection

Each day's prayer meets you right where you are and is a great way for you to begin or end your day.

Read on. . .and be blessed!

GRADUATION DAY

This is the day that the Lord has made.
Let us be full of joy and be glad in it.
PSALM 118:24 NLV

Dear God, this is the day I have waited for—graduation day! Years of education have finally led to a cap, gown, and diploma. Thank You. Thank You for today.

I worked hard, did my best, and now it's time to rejoice and relax. You were with me all the way, Lord, guiding me, teaching me and setting me straight when I strayed. I couldn't have done this without You.

This is the day You made for me—graduation day! Help me to be sensible as I celebrate with my family and friends. Allow my joyfulness and gladness to be a reflection of Your love for me. Remind me that today is not just about me but also about my classmates. Bless them as You have blessed me. Open their eyes to Your goodness.

And now, Father, I pray for tomorrow. As You lead me into the future, help me to walk more closely with You and to stay focused on Your purpose for my life. In Jesus' name, I pray. Amen.

THINK ABOUT IT:
What are your hopes and dreams for the future?

LETTING GO

But Jesus told him, "Anyone who puts
a hand to the plow and then looks back is
not fit for the Kingdom of God."
LUKE 9:62 NLT

Father, letting go is hard. I'm leaving behind a familiar life for an unformed future. I've made friends in school. I've seen them every day, and now it's time to say goodbye. Please remind me that solid friendships survive distance and change. Instill in my friends and myself an attitude of hope as we look forward to our new lives.

I will never forget the good times we've shared. The memories will remain, but I won't look back. Instead, I will set my eyes on what is ahead. A new life awaits me, a life serving You according to Your will. So, Father, ease me gently through the good-byes. Help me to close this chapter of my life story with a song and a smile. Today, I am a graduate. Thank You for that! All the glory goes to You, God. Good-bye to my old life, and hello to the new! Amen.

THINK ABOUT IT:
Is letting go of the past getting in the way of your new beginning?

A NEW BEGINNING

*"For I know the plans I have for you," says
the LORD. "They are plans for good and not for
disaster, to give you a future and a hope."*
JEREMIAH 29:11 NLT

Dear Jesus, I am moving on, about to start a new chapter in my life. New beginnings are both exciting and frightening. The unknown lies before me, and I need reassurance that I'm taking the right path.

God's Word says that His plans for me are already set—good plans with a hopeful future. I believe that!

What I need now is for You to lead me, Jesus. I trust You. Show me the way. As I quiet myself in prayer, speak to me. Clear my mind of any obstacles that keep me from hearing Your voice. Remind me to humble myself before You, to seek Your will and not my own. Calm my fears, and provide me with wisdom to make the right choices. Strengthen my faith as I take the first step into my new life. I'll be ready to begin the journey soon. Hold my hand, Lord. Guide me. Amen.

THINK ABOUT IT:
Reread God's promise in Jeremiah 29:11. Do you trust Him to lead you?

A PILLAR OF CLOUD AND FIRE

The LORD went ahead of them. He guided them
during the day with a pillar of cloud, and he
provided light at night with a pillar of fire.
This allowed them to travel by day or by night.
EXODUS 13:21 NLT

Heavenly Father, as I pray today, I am thinking about the Israelites' exodus from Egypt. You released them from a life of confinement and led them into the wilderness. They relied on their faith and trust in Your promise to guide them.

You went ahead of them, Lord, and they followed You into an ambiguous future. Not only did You go before them, but You made certain that they saw You. You showed them the way with a pillar of clouds in the daytime, with a pillar of fire at night. You never left them alone.

Now I trust You to lead me, Lord. Go before me. Guide me day and night. Open my eyes to Your blessings along the way. Exodus 14:31 says that the Israelites were filled with awe when they saw Your mighty power. Unleash Your power all around me, Lord. I can't wait to see what You have planned for me. Amen.

THINK ABOUT IT:
In what ways do you see the Lord leading you into the future?

KEEP YOUR EYES ON THE PRIZE

I keep trying to reach the goal and get the prize for
which God called me through Christ to the life above.
PHILIPPIANS 3:14 NCV

Dear God, I come to You today in prayer aspiring to be Your faithful servant. I want everything I do to be in accordance with Your will. I have goals in mind for my future, but I wonder if they align with what You want.

What is Your plan for me, Lord? How may I best serve You? I stand at a crossroads now in an ideal place for choosing, so lead me down the right path. Take away any selfish ambitions, and replace them with a firm desire to follow You. Remove all barriers that the enemy puts in my way. Set in my heart Your goals for my future. Then help me to reach those goals.

The prize, Father, is meeting You someday in heaven and hearing You say, "Well done, good and faithful servant!" (Matthew 25:23 NIV). Bless me with wisdom to make the right choices. Help me to keep my eyes on the prize. Amen.

THINK ABOUT IT:
Are you comfortable that your goals align with God's will?

YES, I CAN!

I can do all things because
Christ gives me the strength.
PHILIPPIANS 4:13 NLV

Jesus, I'm worried. To others I might appear confident, but inside I'm anxious. Am I up to the journey? Am I smart enough? Wise enough? I want to succeed in life, but I know that what lies ahead of me is rife with mountains, valleys, bumps, and bruises. There will be detours along the way, tests of my abilities, and even more important tests of my faith. I'm afraid. I worry that maybe I have overestimated my talents and my skills.

But, Lord, Your Word reminds me that I shouldn't worry. I might even have underestimated what I can accomplish. You tell me that I can do *all* things if I trust in You to give me strength. So, Jesus, I relinquish to You my anxiety and insecurity. You are my strength. With You at my side, I can—no, *I will!*—move forward, strong and with confidence. Thank You, dear Lord. Amen.

THINK ABOUT IT:
How can trusting Jesus help ease your mind from worry and lack of confidence?

THANK YOU, GOD!

Humble yourselves before the Lord,
and he will lift you up.
JAMES 4:10 NIV

I'm pleased with my accomplishments, Father. Graduation meant that I achieved a long-awaited goal. I did my best, and all my hard work has led to today and new opportunities.

Graduation day is not all about me. It is more about You and what You did to get me to today. You began teaching me the moment I was born. You made possible simple acts like walking, talking, and learning letters and numbers. You began teaching me life skills: manners, respect, and getting along with others. With each grade in school, You provided me with new abilities, and You refined my talents. You held my hand as we traveled together through the valleys and over the mountains that led to graduation day. You calmed my anxieties and fears.

I believe that You are celebrating graduation with me. You must be so proud of me! All the credit goes to You, God. I love You. Amen.

THINK ABOUT IT:
Have you thanked God and made Him a part of your graduation celebration?

PRAISE GOD!

Praise him for his mighty works;
praise his unequaled greatness!
PSALM 150:2 NLT

Oh, heavenly Father. I have been so preoccupied with celebrating my graduation and looking forward to my future! I want to stop, right now, and thank You for bringing me this far.

When I think of all the years from my birth until now, I am in awe of Your never-ending blessings. Thank You for providing me with my education, teachers and others who have helped along the way, and friends and family who support me, celebrate my successes, and dry my tears when I'm disappointed.

I praise You, Father, for challenging me to exceed my expectations and instilling in me the desire to do my best. I praise You for providing me with courage to try again after I have failed. I'm grateful for my life and for Your promise of a future filled with hope.

Most of all, I want to thank You for all the blessings that I take for granted, the little things You do for me every day. I praise You, my God! Thank You so much. Amen.

THINK ABOUT IT:

Along with prayer and praise, what are other ways that you can honor God?

NEW RELATIONSHIPS

*Don't team up with those who are unbelievers. How
can righteousness be a partner with wickedness?
How can light live with darkness?*
2 CORINTHIANS 6:14 NLT

As I move forward, God, I know that new relationships
are in my future. Some people will become dear and
lifelong friends. Others will challenge me in ways that
are good and not so good.

Inspire me to be kind, understanding, and forgiving
concerning everyone I meet. Help me to guide
unbelievers toward You through my actions and my
words. Remind me to be careful with my relationships
and to not connect too closely with those who do not
love You. I want to live peacefully among nonbelievers,
Father, but I won't accept their ways. I want to always
be an example of righteousness, a shining light for
Christ. Show me how to do that, please. Teach me to
be gentle, like Jesus, and wise in the Word of God.
Lead me to those who will help strengthen my love for
You and also to those who need to know You. In Jesus'
name, I pray. Amen.

THINK ABOUT IT:
What qualities are you looking for in new relationships?

IT'S OKAY TO ASK FOR HELP

*Plans fail without good advice, but they
succeed with the advice of many others.*
PROVERBS 15:22 NCV

Father, sometimes I make the mistake of thinking that being an adult means having enough self-confidence that I shouldn't need to ask for help. I know that's flawed thinking. Everyone needs help. Proverbs 15:22 confirms it—plans fail without good advice.

Lord, Your Word encourages me to seek the counsel of many others. So whenever I need assistance, lead me to wise believers. If I hesitate to seek advice, speak to my heart and remind me that it's okay to ask for help. I won't allow my pride to get in the way. Teach me to discern between those who provide guidance in accordance with Your will and those who are worldly or might be self-serving. Show me how to put wise advice to the best use as I move forward. Lead me to succeed in all that I do for You, not for my recognition, Father, but for Your glory. Amen.

THINK ABOUT IT:
Is pride or worrying about how others might perceive you getting in the way of you asking for help?

WHO'S THE BOSS?

Work with enthusiasm, as though you were working for the Lord rather than for people.
EPHESIANS 6:7 NLT

Dear God, it is easy for me to forget whom I work for, whom I serve. I've always tried to do my best to please my family, teachers, coaches, bosses, and myself. I've worked hard and with enthusiasm to reach my goals and do a good job. I've often celebrated my successes. But, heavenly Father, hard work isn't worthy of celebration unless that work is for You.

I want everything I work for to honor You, to bring myself and others closer to You. Whether my work is an important assignment or a mundane task, I want to do it joyfully, remembering that You are the one in charge.

You are a good boss—the best kind. You encourage me, support me, and even love me! The men and women I work for, now and in the future, might challenge my worth, ability, and patience. But, Father, I won't let that discourage me. Instead, I will set my thoughts on pleasing You. Amen.

THINK ABOUT IT:
Will you serve God above all others?

JUST THIS ONCE

"And lead us not into temptation,
but deliver us from the evil one."
MATTHEW 6:13 NIV

Jesus, You warned me not to slip into temptation. But sometimes the evil one is skilled at wrapping what is bad for me in an attractive package. New experiences await me, and I don't want naïveté to cause me to fall. I need You.

As I face each new freedom, encourage me to choose wisely in accordance with Your will. Protect me from tripping into traps, such as immorality, unethical behavior, selfishness, and crude language. Especially, help me to remember that *just this once* often leads to a lifetime of giving in to temptation.

When I find myself attracted to something that I know is wrong, never allow me to forget that You are my strength. Give me power to stand firm and stand up for what I know is right. I want each new experience and challenge to make me wise and bring me closer to You. Jesus, my faith and my trust are in You. Amen.

THINK ABOUT IT:
What temptations do you find difficult to resist?

FIRST IMPRESSIONS

Do you think I am trying to make people accept me?
No, God is the One I am trying to please. Am I trying
to please people? If I still wanted to please people,
I would not be a servant of Christ.
GALATIANS 1:10 NCV

Lord, hear my prayer. I'm about to start a new adventure. On every road I travel, I will meet strangers along the way, and I want to make a good first impression.

At times, I might be tempted to win a person's acceptance by acting like someone I'm not. Help me to be myself—a child of God and a servant of Christ—with each new person I meet.

When I encounter someone new, I will do my best to act the way Jesus would. I will be welcoming, gentle, and kind, yet always strong in my faith and commitment to You. Instead of working to please a job interviewer, teacher, new boss, or coworker, I will concentrate on pleasing You. And if someone chooses not to accept me, I won't allow their actions to discourage me. What's important, Father, is that You accept me. And You do! Always. Just as I am. Amen.

THINK ABOUT IT:
Have you made a plan for how you will behave toward the strangers you meet?

BLESS MY FINANCES

*And my God will meet all your needs according
to the riches of his glory in Christ Jesus.*
PHILIPPIANS 4:19 NIV

Heavenly Father, I have financial responsibilities now,
things like insurance, tuition, transportation, supplies
and clothing for work and school. . . . I worry about
making ends meet. I need to budget wisely and watch
my spending. But even if I'm careful, Lord, will I have
enough?

Your Word tells me that You promise to meet *all*
my needs. That word *all* is so important. It means
that I shouldn't worry about anything because You
understand exactly what I need all the time. I have to
remember that.

I will commit Philippians 4:19 to memory and
recall it often. You are my Father. You will take care of
me! I believe with all my heart that You will provide
for my finances as I take this next big step in my life.

I'm grateful for Your provisions, now and each and
every day, and I know that I am already rich in spirit
because You love me. Amen.

THINK ABOUT IT:
Do you think spending wisely honors God? (Read
Matthew 19:24.)

LET'S GET SERIOUS

*Whoever listens to what is taught will succeed,
and whoever trusts the LORD will be happy.*
PROVERBS 16:20 NCV

Dear God, graduation comes with a soaring sense of freedom. I can't wait to have amazing experiences, meet new people, and move forward with my life. This is an exciting time filled with possibility.

I understand that if I want to be successful, it is essential that I stay on course and keep my mind fixed on You. The enemy will put worldly distractions in my way. Please help me to be aware of these potential distractions.

I want to have fun and be happy with my newfound freedom, but I need to spend my time wisely. Allow me to be serious about learning new skills and growing in maturity so I may succeed in ways that make You proud. Guide and teach me to do what is right and good. Father, grant me the ability to stay focused on the future as I put my faith and trust in You. In Christ's name, I pray. Amen.

THINK ABOUT IT:
Will you stay focused on God when distractions get in your way?

TRANSFORMATION

*This means that anyone who belongs to Christ
has become a new person. The old life is
gone; a new life has begun!*
2 CORINTHIANS 5:17 NLT

Today, Lord, I am reflecting on the people and experiences You've provided me throughout my life. With each passing year, I grew in knowledge and spirit. Through guidance from my family and teachers, I polished the talents and abilities You blessed me with. I learned about relationships, how to love, how to forgive, and how to let go. You made me laugh and smile, Lord, as I shared fun times with my friends.

And now, You've brought me here—my old life is gone; a new life has begun!

Graduation brings sad tears as life in the present becomes a memory. But there are happy tears, too! You are about to transform me into a new person, an even better person than I am right now. Who will I be in five years? Ten? Or twenty-five? Only You know, God. But one thing is certain, one thing will never change—now and forever I am Yours, a child of the living God. Amen.

THINK ABOUT IT:

As a graduate, have you felt the Lord beginning to change you?

AIM FOR THE STARS

*"And when you look up into the sky and see the sun,
moon, and stars—all the forces of heaven—don't be
seduced into worshiping them. The Lord your God
gave them to all the peoples of the earth."*
DEUTERONOMY 4:19 NLT

When I look at the stars, God, I see Your greatness. I
think of Genesis 15:5 (NIV) when You took Abraham
outside and said, "Look up at the sky and count the
stars—if indeed you can count them." You said to him,
"So shall your offspring be." I remember Psalm 147:4
that tells me You know each star by name. When I
look at the stars, Father, I see countless possibilities
for my future. I want to reach higher and higher—to
be successful, to aim for the stars!

I know that success often leads to pride, and I
don't want to be seduced into worshipping the rewards
my achievements might bring. Please guide me to be
successful in my work, but keep me humble. If Your
plan is for me to lead, then make me into a leader who
not only encourages others to be successful, but who
also leads them to You. Amen.

THINK ABOUT IT:
What character traits do you think God expects from
one who leads?

I'M NOT PERFECT

Moses said to the Lord, "Pardon your servant, Lord.
I have never been eloquent, neither in the past
nor since you have spoken to your servant.
I am slow of speech and tongue."
EXODUS 4:10 NIV

Heavenly Father, what lies ahead of me seems so vast it's overwhelming. What if more is expected of me than I'm able to do? I'm not perfect, after all, but sometimes I feel like I have to be. It's during those times, Father, that I need You to remind me of Moses.

He wasn't perfect either. Moses didn't speak well, and he worried about how the Israelites would perceive him as their leader. Would they listen to his less-than-perfect words, or laugh at him and think of him as a fool?

You encouraged Moses to put all his faith in You and step beyond his comfort level. You gave him the strength he needed to believe that he was able—because his trust was in You.

I'm not perfect, Lord. But I trust You. In times of doubt, I believe that You will lead me, just as You did Moses, to carry out whatever You have planned for me. Amen.

THINK ABOUT IT:
Is something in the way of you moving beyond your comfort level?

A WORD FROM THE WISE

*My child, listen to your father's teaching
and do not forget your mother's advice.*
PROVERBS 1:8 NCV

Lord, thank You for the older adults in my life, those You have put in place to guide me.

Parents, grandparents, aunts, uncles—they are farther along life's journey than I am, and they provide wisdom gained from their successes as well as their failures. Thank You for their support and encouragement. And, especially, thank You for those times when they have shown me by their example how to serve You and others.

Lord, take away any pride that gets in the way of me asking for their opinions.

At times, I have avoided their guidance, choosing instead to go my own way. Help me, please, to think about their advice and to weigh their counsel against Your Word.

Lead me also to seek out older adults who are wise in Your Word so that I might learn more about You and Your ways. In Jesus' name, I pray. Amen.

THINK ABOUT IT:
How have the older adults in your life helped you grow closer to God?

I MIGHT BE YOUNG, BUT. . .

Let no one show little respect for you because you are
young. Show other Christians how to live by your life.
They should be able to follow you in the way you
talk and in what you do. Show them how to live
in faith and in love and in holy living.
1 TIMOTHY 4:12 NLV

Dear God, let me be an example of Christ to everyone
I meet. I might be young, but in my words and actions,
I can be like Jesus.

Help me to model strength against evil. I think
of young David, the shepherd boy, who stood up to
the giant Philistine soldier, Goliath, when even the
bravest of Israelite soldiers were afraid. And I think
of Jesus—still a young man—the One who accepted
Your will despite suffering and pain.

The New Testament tells of the boy who gave
Jesus his lunch, just bread and fish, trusting Christ to
do with it as He wanted. Allow me to be generous like
that and to share what I have.

Remind me to speak gently and respectfully and
to never be shy about sharing my faith with others.
I might be young, Lord, but still, I am Your servant,
growing in wisdom every day. Amen.

THINK ABOUT IT:
In what ways can you show others how to live in faith,
love, and holiness?

TEACH ME TO PRAY

*And it came to pass, that, as he was praying in
a certain place, when he ceased, one of his
disciples said unto him, Lord, teach us to pray,
as John also taught his disciples.*

LUKE 11:1 KJV

Heavenly Father, when I come to You in prayer,
sometimes I can't find the right words. Certainly, You
know all my wants and needs even when I can't express
them. The Bible tells me that the Holy Spirit will pray
for me in those times, and You, Father, who knows my
heart, will know what the Spirit is saying (Romans
8:26–27).

And when I can't find the words, God, then I can
always pray as Jesus taught us to pray:

"Our Father which art in heaven, Hallowed be thy
name. Thy kingdom come, Thy will be done in earth,
as it is in heaven. Give us this day our daily bread. And
forgive us our debts, as we forgive our debtors. And
lead us not into temptation, but deliver us from evil:
For thine is the kingdom, and the power, and the glory,
for ever" (Matthew 6:9–13 KJV).

Thank You, Father, for helping me to pray. Amen.

THINK ABOUT IT:
When you couldn't find the words to pray, did you ask
the Holy Spirit for help?

THE INTERVIEW

May the favor of the Lord our God rest on us;
establish the work of our hands for us—yes,
establish the work of our hands.
PSALM 90:17 NIV

God, I need You. Please hear my prayer.

Guide me as I look for work. Lead me bravely into each job interview. Take away my anxiety and replace it with Your peace. Allow me to make a good first impression through my appearance, actions, and words. Help me to present my genuine self—the me You created—instead of trying to impress by being someone I'm not.

Thank You for the skills and talents You have given me. Help me to speak of my strengths with confidence and of my weaknesses with humility and a willingness to learn.

I know that You have the perfect job for me, so I will not be discouraged. I will continue seeking work with faith, trusting in You, knowing that You alone direct my path. Thank You, Father. Amen.

THINK ABOUT IT:
What are the first and last things you should do when preparing for a job interview?

SEND ME AARONS AND HURS

*When Moses' hands grew tired, they took a stone
and put it under him and he sat on it. Aaron and Hur
held his hands up—one on one side, one on the other—
so that his hands remained steady till sunset.*

EXODUS 17:12 NIV

Letting go and moving forward can feel like a losing
battle, Lord. I sometimes take one step into the future,
and then life gets in the way. Like in a game, I'm sent
back to "go."

The Bible tells a story about Moses and the
Israelites facing a battle with their enemy, the
Amalekites. Moses stood atop a hill watching Joshua
and his people fight against the enemy. As long as
Moses held up his hands, Joshua's soldiers won the
battle; but when he let down his hands, the Amalekites
prospered. When Moses' hands grew tired, his friends
Aaron and Hur held them up. They held up Moses'
weary hands until the Israelites won!

Father, I need faithful friends like that. Send me
God-loving friends—Aarons and Hurs—to hold up my
hands when I feel like I can't go on. Help me to meet
each challenge with faith instead of despair. Amen.

THINK ABOUT IT:
Whom can you count on to "hold up your hands"?

GOLD APPLES IN A SILVER BOWL

"For by your words you will be acquitted,
and by your words you will be condemned."
MATTHEW 12:37 NIV

Dear Lord, as I move forward in life, I'm discovering the importance of good communication. I'm so used to communicating quickly, like when I text, that I've become lazy about choosing my words wisely, both in writing and in speaking.

I know that communicating well is an important skill, especially in the workplace. So, I'm asking You to remind me to think about my words. Help me not to respond so quickly that I sound harsh and uncaring. Encourage me to take time to listen and to answer in a way that lifts others up instead of bringing them down. Provide me with the ability to convey instructions clearly instead of carelessly and to always be respectful. Your Word says, "The right word spoken at the right time is as beautiful as gold apples in a silver bowl" (Proverbs 25:11 NCV). Please teach me to use the right words at the right times.

Thank You, dear Lord, for loving me and for caring about everything I do. Amen.

THINK ABOUT IT:
How can you improve your communication skills so you will be a godly example to others?

HAVE FUN!

*So I recommend having fun, because there is
nothing better for people in this world than to eat,
drink, and enjoy life. That way they will experience
some happiness along with all the hard work
God gives them under the sun.*
ECCLESIASTES 8:15 NLT

Heavenly Father, thank You for good times, play, and lazy days spent in the sun. Thank You for vacations and new things to do and see. Thank You for celebrations, smiles, laughter, music, dancing. . .an almost endless assortment of things to do. Thank You for Christian friends to hang out with.

I'm so grateful to You for the opportunity to live and enjoy life's godly pleasures. You bless me with joyfulness, and often in the most unexpected circumstances. I love Your little surprises, those spontaneous times that give me a happy heart.

You always know when it's the perfect time for me to let go of my concerns and have a little fun. So, when I feel You nudging me to take a break and relax a bit, I will listen. I will remember that it's okay with You that I not be serious all the time. Thank You, God. Amen.

THINK ABOUT IT:
Can you think of a recent time when God blessed you with some unexpected fun?

A PRAYER AND A PLAN

*There is a time for everything, and everything
on earth has its special season.*
ECCLESIASTES 3:1 NCV

God, I want to be productive and use my time wisely. Ecclesiastes 3:1 reminds me that there is a time for everything—if I don't waste it.

I need to limit the minutes I spend on my phone and social media. It's so easy, Father, to lose track of time if I'm texting or doing other things online. Guide me to start every day with a prayer and a plan, and then to stick to it.

Help me to discern the most important tasks and then prioritize them. Keep my mind on what I need to do, and lead me away from nonproductive thoughts that can be emotionally draining. If I worry about not getting everything done, remind me that You are in control; maybe You have a different plan for my day than the one that I've made. Inspire me to work hard but also to take time for myself, and especially to make time for You! In Jesus' name, I pray. Amen.

THINK ABOUT IT:
Do you start each day with a prayer and a plan?

READY, WILLING, AND WAITING

*But they who wait upon the Lord will get new
strength. They will rise up with wings like
eagles. They will run and not get tired.
They will walk and not become weak.*

ISAIAH 40:31 NLV

Heavenly Father, I'm ready to get moving, to go out into
the world and start my new life. Is that what You want—
for me to hurry up and get going? I'm unsure what to
do next, and I feel anxious. I want to do something,
but I can't make up my mind about what. When I pray
and ask You for direction, You are silent. Why, Lord?
Surely, You know how eager I am to get on with my
life. I'm waiting. Tell me what to do.

I wonder: Are You the One waiting for me? Maybe
what You want from me is patience.

Father, help me to wait patiently for Your directions.
Bless me with a sense of contentment where I am
right now. I know I'm okay; I'm okay in this moment,
exactly where You have me. So, I will do my best to
wait patiently instead of rushing ahead of You. Amen.

THINK ABOUT IT:

Ecclesiastes 7:8 (NLT) says, "Finishing is better than
starting. Patience is better than pride." What do you
think this means?

BABY STEPS

*The LORD makes firm the steps of the one who
delights in him; though he may stumble, he will not
fall, for the LORD upholds him with his hand.*
PSALM 37:23-24 NIV

Dear God, beginning a new life chapter is much like
learning to walk. I tentatively take my first step forward.
I might stumble, but with You watching over me I will
never fall. If I feel unsteady, I know that I can grab hold
of Your hand and You will help me—baby steps—one
foot in front of the other—until I am sure that my legs
are strong enough to carry me.

Oh, God. You are so good to me! My delight is in
You. I trust that You will never leave me. As I begin this
new adventure, You are with me on straight, smooth
roads and rocky paths, through valleys and over
mountains. When I grow weary, I know that You will
carry me. Wherever I go, I will not be afraid because
You are my guide.

Thank You for accompanying me on this journey,
Lord. Here we go, one step at a time. Amen.

THINK ABOUT IT:
How do you know that God is always with you?

I'M NOT THAT PERSON ANYMORE

We have freedom now,
because Christ made us free.
GALATIANS 5:1 NCV

I'm in a place, Lord, where I have to redefine who I am. So much of my identity has been linked to school—learning, grades, friends, and activities. But I'm not that person anymore. Whether I wanted to or not, I've left that all behind. You've set me free and made my life a clean slate.

One thing that hasn't changed is that I am Yours. I believe that just as You led Your children, the Israelites, to their Promised Land, You will lead me to mine. I am Your child, and You will care for me.

Reinvent me, Lord. Help me to grow in maturity. Fill my slate with the wisdom found in Your Word. Wherever I go, give me a spirit that bears "good fruit"—love, joy, peace, patience, kindness, goodness, faithfulness, gentleness, and self-control. Create in me a clean heart, and steer me clear of temptation.

I want my new self to be more like You. Amen.

THINK ABOUT IT:
What about you would you like to change as you begin this new phase of your life?

WHAT IF THEY DON'T LIKE ME?

When I saw their fear, I got up and said to the
rulers and leaders and the rest of the people,
"Do not be afraid of them. Remember the Lord
Who is great and honored with fear. And fight
for your brothers, your sons, your daughters,
your wives, and your houses."

NEHEMIAH 4:14 NLV

Dear Jesus. It's hard being a Christian in a world filled with sin. But this is nothing new. Your servant, Paul, suffered because of his faith; still he held firm. When others ridiculed him for believing in You, he didn't question whether You exist. Instead, his faith grew stronger. He fought for his Christian beliefs by never giving up. Even when he was in prison, Paul continued working for You. He taught younger believers, like Timothy, to grow in their faith; he encouraged church leaders in Rome, Corinth, Ephesus, Philippi. . .and he prayed for nonbelievers everywhere.

Jesus, as I walk this new road, I know I will encounter those who hate and reject me because of my faith. I will not be afraid of them! Help me to react like Paul—to be gentle yet firm in my Christian beliefs and never, ever hide my love for You. Amen.

THINK ABOUT IT:
How will you react if you encounter hate because of your Christian beliefs?

WITH A LITTLE HELP FROM MY FRIENDS

The godly give good advice to their friends.
PROVERBS 12:26 NLT

Dear God, sometimes I don't take time to really think things through. I forge ahead on a new path and discover that it's a dead end. Then I'm in a mess. Trying to get out of a mess can tangle it more. It upsets me when I allow myself to be so careless.

You have blessed me with good Christian friends who will help me. Talking things through with them is one way to untangle a mess. But, God, remind me to be sensitive to whether their advice aligns with Your will.

I think of Job's friends in the Bible. They were godly men with good intentions, but their advice was not in line with what You wanted for Job.

When I get into a mess and ask for advice from my friends, I will request that we pray together to discover Your plan for me. I will remember Christ's words in Matthew 18:20 (NLT)—"For where two or three gather together as my followers, I am there among them." Amen.

THINK ABOUT IT:
Do you and your friends pray for each other to discern God's will?

WHAT AM I REALLY AFRAID OF?

I asked the LORD for help, and he answered me.
He saved me from all that I feared.
PSALM 34:4 NCV

Heavenly Father, I feel anxious a lot. I don't know why, but I'm just on edge. The future is ahead of me, a clean slate. I'm excited wondering where I will go and what new adventures await me. But mixed in with the excitement is fear. I've tried to discover exactly what it is that I'm afraid of, but I can't seem to identify it. I don't like feeling this way. I want to settle my emotions and find peace.

Here I am, Lord! Let's spend time together. Please quiet my anxiety. Fill my soul with Your presence, and save me from all my fears. I know that You love me. You are with me always. Nothing that I'm afraid of can hurt me because You are greater than whatever I fear. So, help me to relax. Invite me to rest in Your arms for a while, serene and unafraid. Amen.

THINK ABOUT IT:
What *are* you really afraid of?

SEE IT. SAY IT. DO IT.

Do not merely listen to the word,
and so deceive yourselves. Do what it says.
JAMES 1:22 NIV

Thank You, God, for the Bible. As I study Your Word, I know that I am growing in godly wisdom. I do my best not only to read the Bible but also to memorize key verses. The stories I read about people in the Bible aid me in learning about my own self and how I interact with others. But I need to take my Bible study one step further. It is not enough just to become familiar with Your Word and memorize scripture. I need to do it!

Second Timothy 3:16 (NCV) says that "all Scripture is inspired by [You] and is useful for teaching, for showing people what is wrong in their lives, for correcting faults, and for teaching how to live right." Help me, Father, to apply what I learn from the Bible— to put it into practice in my everyday life. As I do this, I know that I will grow not only in wisdom but also in my faith and service to You. Amen.

THINK ABOUT IT:
Do you apply scripture to your everyday life?

BEYOND MY EXPECTATIONS

God is able to do much more than we ask or think through His power working in us.
EPHESIANS 3:20 NLV

Father, why do I worry about not reaching my goals? As long as I advance according to Your plan for me, I can accomplish far more than what I expect. The key thing for me to remember is that I am not motivated to exceed my objectives for my own glory but for Yours! Together, we will work Your plan.

I see Your greatness all around me as I look at the works of Your hands—the sky, mountains, oceans. . . . Awe fills me whenever I hear about the miracles You still perform—healing cancers and other illnesses in the body, rescuing people from accidents that might have taken their lives, providing unexpected money in a financial crisis. . . . Your brilliance exceeds anything I can imagine.

So, Lord, when I think I can't, I will remember that I *can*! With Your power working within me, I can achieve great things for You. And, God, the glory is all Yours. Amen.

THINK ABOUT IT:
Can you recall a time when God helped you to exceed your expectations?

WHEN MY PLAN DOESN'T WORK

This is what the LORD says: "Stop at the crossroads and look around. Ask for the old, godly way, and walk in it. Travel its path, and you will find rest for your souls. But you reply, 'No, that's not the road we want!'"
JEREMIAH 6:16 NLT

Dear God, nothing I've planned for my future is working out as I thought it would. Why have You closed so many doors that I had hoped to enter? Why have You stopped me from moving forward? Here I am wandering on a path to nowhere.

In Jeremiah 6:16, You tell me to look around. Ask for instructions. Walk in a godly way. I've tried that, Father, but I must be going in the wrong direction, because I feel frustrated, weary, and confused.

You know the desires of my heart. You understand that I've had my heart set on walking this path. So why, Lord? Why have You stopped me?

I don't want to take a new road, but I will if that is what You want from me. I will put all my trust in You. Lead me to the road You want me to take. Help me to surrender my desires. And, God—please give my soul some rest. Amen.

THINK ABOUT IT:
How do you react when God closes the door on something you'd hoped for?

LET'S PARTY!

*Those who do not know God are surprised you do not
join them in the sinful things they do. They laugh
at you and say bad things against you.*
1 PETER 4:4 NLV

Graduation means parties, Lord, and new freedoms. I
want to enjoy celebrating with my former classmates,
but I don't want to slip into sin while having fun.

A few of my friends are nonbelievers, and I don't
agree with some of the things they do. It's difficult for
me, at times, to decide whether to look away or walk
away. Give me wisdom to know what to do. And if they
make fun of me for not joining in, then help me to react
in a firm yet gentle and godly way.

I won't take part in anything that doesn't glorify
You, Lord. I will never deny You or my faith, but instead,
I will leave a party if things happen there that I know
You disapprove of.

I know that You want me to celebrate my
graduation, be joyful, and have fun. I promise to do
that, Lord, in ways that honor You. Amen.

THINK ABOUT IT:
Do you and your friends party in a way that honors God?

GOD, WHERE ARE YOU?

Come near to God,
and he will come near to you.
JAMES 4:8 CEV

Dear God, I've just realized that I've been ignoring You lately. Please forgive me. I've been so busy that I've not paid enough attention to my relationship with You. Now You seem so far away. You haven't left me, God, have You? I trust that You are always with me, but now You are silent. Please speak to me again as I read my Bible, meditate on scripture, and pray.

I know that You should always be my first priority, especially when life gets busy and I scramble to get everything done. Why is it so easy for me to forget that? I love You, God, and I'm sorry for not telling You that more often, not only with my words, but also through my actions.

Here I am, Lord. Please come near to me. Let's spend time together. I want to tell You about what I've been doing and ask for Your guidance. Amen.

THINK ABOUT IT:
Is your relationship with God your first priority even when you are busy?

MY TOTALLY AWESOME GOD

*Nothing in all creation is hidden from God's sight.
Everything is uncovered and laid bare before the
eyes of him to whom we must give account.*
HEBREWS 4:13 NIV

Heavenly Father, You are so amazing! The world has more than seven billion people. I am like a speck among them; yet You know everything about me, even the smallest details. You know how many hairs are on my head (Matthew 10:30). You see when I cry, and You count my tears (Psalm 56:8).

My ability is limited, but Yours is infinite. You are all-knowing and all-seeing all the time! In this crowded and busy world, nothing happens in my life without Your eyes seeing it. Your hand is in everything. You keep track of each step I take, and if I stumble, You steady me and make sure that I don't fall.

Oh, Lord, Your awesomeness is so far beyond anything that I can understand. You are so big, and I am so small and insignificant in the world. Still, I am important to You, and You love me. Thank You! I love You, too. Amen.

THINK ABOUT IT:
God sees everything. Have you been trying to hide something from Him?

QUESTIONS WITHOUT ANSWERS

The secret things belong to the LORD our God,
but the things revealed belong to us and
to our children forever, that we may
follow all the words of this law.
DEUTERONOMY 29:29 NIV

I have so many questions for You, God. I wish that I could look ten years into the future and know where I will be. I want to know Your plans for me, all of them. But You withhold answers to such things. You keep many of Your reasons and ways secret.

Yes, I have unanswered questions; still, the more I read and meditate on Your Word, the greater my understanding becomes. Through the Bible, You reveal to me all the things You want me to know. As I dig deeper into scripture, my faith grows stronger. And with faith, God, my unanswered questions don't seem so important anymore. My trust is in You. I believe that You have everything in my life under control, even when through my eyes it appears chaotic. Right now, it is enough for me to know that I am Your child and You love me. Amen.

THINK ABOUT IT:
What one question do you wish God would answer?

PERSPIRE TO ASPIRE!

You lazy people can learn by watching an anthill.
Ants don't have leaders, but they store up
food during harvest season. How long
will you lie there doing nothing at all?
PROVERBS 6:6-9 CEV

Dear Father, I've worked hard to get this far. And now that I've graduated, there is a part of me that just wants to relax. There's nothing wrong with taking a little break, but I don't want to become lazy. I know that succeeding in the next phase of my life will take a lot of hard work. So, refresh me, Lord. Get me ready to work again.

When in school, I got used to people telling me what to do and holding me accountable. Now I am responsible for me! I need to set my mind on working diligently toward my goals.

If I get tired and feel like quitting, You will be my strength. Protect me from slipping into self-pity when the work becomes hard. Bless me with enthusiasm and determination to get going and keep going. Help me to remember that You are my leader, my boss, and that everything I do is for You. Amen.

THINK ABOUT IT:
How do you handle hard work?

HARD TO SAY GOOD-BYE

"Go in peace, for we have sworn friendship with each other in the name of the LORD, saying, 'The LORD is witness between you and me, and between your descendants and my descendants forever.'"
1 SAMUEL 20:42 NIV

Lord, I'm eager to move on, but I don't want to leave behind the people I love. I worry that my relationships with my best friends will weaken or that we will grow apart and not see each other again. I feel sad when I think about it.

Your Word says there is a time for everything (Ecclesiastes 3:1). You have blessed me with the greatest friends! The time I spend with them is precious. Together we've created fun traditions and happy memories. I want that to continue. I don't want a time to come when we have to say good-bye.

Life is changing for my friends and me, but I ask that You will keep our friendships strong. Watch over us as we go our own ways, and bless us. Allow us to walk together on this road to maturity and, please, grant us the gift of being best friends forever. Thank You, Lord. Amen.

THINK ABOUT IT:
Can you think of examples of friendship in the Bible? What do you think made those friendships strong?

CLIMB TO THE TOP

[Jacob] had a dream in which he saw a stairway
resting on the earth, with its top reaching to
heaven, and the angels of God were ascending
and descending on it. There above it stood the
LORD, and he said: "I am the LORD, the God of
your father Abraham and the God of Isaac."
GENESIS 28:12–13 NIV

Father, I feel like I am about to climb an infinite flight of stairs. I have no idea where they lead, and I'm a little bit afraid. Maybe I will find my hopes and dreams at the top, or maybe You have a completely different plan for me.

One footstep at a time, I begin the ascent. My steps might be tentative at first, but as I build my faith and trust in You, I know that I will climb each stair with confidence.

I think of the Bible story about Jacob. In his dream, he saw a stairway leading to heaven, and You were at the top.

My climb might be long, Father. Maybe it will be a difficult one. For now, everything I encounter along the way is Your secret. But I know that when I get to the top—the place where I realize Your plan for me—You will be there waiting. That alone is enough to make me eager to begin the climb. Amen.

THINK ABOUT IT:
What is the first step you plan to take in your post-graduation journey?

THERE'S TROUBLE AHEAD

"I have told you these things so you may have peace in Me. In the world you will have much trouble. But take hope! I have power over the world!"
JOHN 16:33 NLV

Dear God, I don't expect life to be trouble free. I believe there will be challenges along the way. I don't like to think about the disturbing events I might face; still, I want to make a plan for how I will react when they happen.

Remind me, God, to make You the center of my life. Plant Yourself so firmly in my heart that I can't miss feeling You there. And when trouble comes, strengthen my faith in You. Help me to remember that there is nothing You cannot do. You have power over any difficulty or danger that gets in my way.

When life turns messy, instill in me a sense of peace. Lead me to surrender my problems to You and then rest knowing that You will guide me through them. Give me the ability to stay levelheaded in a crisis. Keep me from slipping into worry and fear. Thank You, Father. In Jesus' name, I pray. Amen.

THINK ABOUT IT:
What can you do right now that will help you prepare for trouble in the future?

WORTHLESS THINGS

Keep me from looking at worthless things.
Let me live by your word.
PSALM 119:37 NCV

Heavenly Father, I think every graduate wants to be successful and earn a good salary. I'm no different. I think about landing a great job with a big paycheck. I allow myself to think of all the things I could have if only I had enough money. Forgive me.

Help me, God, to keep my thoughts from slipping into dreams of wealth and possessions. I trust that You will provide for all my needs according to Your will. My relationship with You is priceless. Compared with that, everything else is worthless.

Success will come to me when I live according to Your Word. If You decide to bless me with money, then I will honor You by spending wisely and giving generously. And if my paychecks are not as big as I would like them to be, I promise to be content with what I have. You, Lord, are my everything. You are enough. Amen.

THINK ABOUT IT:

Is your relationship with God more important to you than money and possessions?

COMMENCEMENT BLUES

A happy heart is like good medicine,
but a broken spirit drains your strength.
PROVERBS 17:22 NCV

God, sometimes, I don't know what I want to do. I think I have a plan to start my new life, and then I get overwhelmed. My emotions are all over the place. That alone is exhausting.

Freedom is mine! I love having options to consider. I completed my studies, and I graduated. So, why do I feel so confused and sad?

Will You help me to stay positive? Give me a happy heart. I have so much to be grateful for. You've blessed me beyond my expectations. You've wiped my slate clean and given me a fresh start.

I will think about all You have done and be happy because You love me. Turn my frowns into smiles! Fill my heart with Your love overflowing; then lead me to share it with others. I believe that happiness is contagious, and if I am happy, I will lift the spirits of everyone around me. Pick me up, Lord. Let me be a reflection of Your love. Amen.

THINK ABOUT IT:
If your spirit is broken, what can you do to mend it?

THE CROWDED HIGHWAY

*When the king sent the people out of Egypt,
God did not lead them on the road through
the Philistine country, though that was the
shortest way. . . . God led them through
the desert toward the Red Sea.*
EXODUS 13:17–18 NCV

Dear Lord, as I begin this new journey, I'm discovering that the road is crowded with recent graduates. We're all sprinting toward new opportunities and seeking the shortest path. The problem for me, Lord, is that I'm not sure I want to stay on this road in the fast lane. What do You want me to do?

I remember that when You led the Israelites out of Egypt, You didn't lead them by the shortest way. Instead, You led them for forty years through the desert. At the end of the long road, they received the land that You had promised them.

I know that the shortest route is not always the best. Should I stay on this crowded highway, or do You want me to take a road less traveled? Speak to me, Lord. I've quieted my thoughts, and I'm listening. I am willing and ready to follow wherever You lead me. Amen.

THINK ABOUT IT:
Are you ready if God chooses to lead you on a long road to reach your goals?

I THANK GOD FOR YOU!

I thank God for you whenever I think of you.
I always have joy as I pray for all of you.
PHILIPPIANS 1:3–4 NLV

Heavenly Father, as I pray today, I am thinking of all the people who encouraged me on the way to graduation. Family, friends, teachers, even a stranger or two, helped in ways big and small. I'm grateful for them. I'm thankful for church leaders and friends who mentored me in reading and understanding Your Word. I appreciate every card and gift I received at graduation and those who took time to celebrate with me.

I've been busy, Lord, but I need to stop and let all these wonderful people know how much I value them. I've thanked You for them, but I may have neglected to tell them what they mean to me and how they've helped me to get where I am today.

Provide me with the words to thank them. Bless them, Father, in all that they do. As I move forward in life, please continue to put me together with people like them, and also lead me to help others as they have helped me. In Jesus' name, I pray. Amen.

THINK ABOUT IT:
Make a list of people who helped lead you toward graduation. Have you thanked them?

DON'T JUDGE

"Do not judge, or you too will be judged.
For in the same way you judge others,
you will be judged, and with the measure
you use, it will be measured to you."
MATTHEW 7:1-2 NIV

Dear Jesus, as I move forward in life, I need to think about Your words in Matthew 7:1-2. I don't mean to—and sometimes I am not even aware that I am doing it—but I confess that I have judged others because of their actions and words. I've judged them on first impressions, too, and even appearance. I've forgotten that judgment is Yours, Lord, and not mine.

I am careful not to become too close with those who don't believe in You (2 Corinthians 6:14), but I can be a good example to them, by loving them as You would. God gives everyone freedom to live as they choose. So, instead of judging others, I can pray for them and ask You to lead them to choose and honor You.

Help me to be gentle in my opinions about others and not to speak badly of them. Teach me to act toward them the way that You would. Amen.

THINK ABOUT IT:
Do you judge others? How do you think God wants you to treat them?

STRONG ROOTS

*In those days I was strong like a tree
with deep roots and with plenty of water.*
JOB 29:19 CEV

Father God, in some ways I feel alone. What lies ahead is uncertain. When I was in school, I knew that teachers, family, friends, and others were there to support me whenever I needed help. But now I am expected to make my own rules and follow them and to rely more on myself than on others. I'm a little afraid to leave that old support system behind.

You are my roots, and I trust that You will help me to grow strong as I begin this new chapter in my life. Please build my confidence in You, Lord, and help me also to build confidence in myself as I learn to follow You. Provide me with a new support system of Christian friends whom I can count on when I need help. Remind me not to be afraid and never to feel alone, because You are always with me. Thank You, God. Amen.

THINK ABOUT IT:
God provides the roots from which you grow. Who are the branches—the ones you trust to support you?

LEAVING HOME

And Ruth said, Intreat me not to leave thee,
or to return from following after thee: for whither
thou goest, I will go; and where thou lodgest,
I will lodge: thy people shall be my
people, and thy God my God.
RUTH 1:16 KJV

Lord, everyone has to leave home, and now it's my turn. Bittersweet is how I feel. Sadness about leaving behind what is so familiar mixes with feelings of excitement and anticipation.

Leaving home isn't easy. Home pulls hard wanting me to stay. But I know that I have to move toward what lies ahead.

Wherever I go, I know that You will be with me. That idea comforts me. My family will be with me too in spirit. I might not live with them anymore, but they will always be in my heart and eager for my visits. I will take along with me all their love.

Home is where I've felt safe, Lord. I'm leaving behind familiar rooms and predictable routines for everything new. But I know that I am safe with You wherever I go. Lead me into my future. Wherever You take me, I am at home with You. Amen.

THINK ABOUT IT:
How can your faith in God help when you leave home?

MOM AND DAD

"Honor your father and your mother,
as the Lord your God has told you."
DEUTERONOMY 5:16 NLV

Thank You, God, for my parents. They've put up with a lot from me as I've grown and changed. Our relationship has had its ups and downs, but through it all I've known that they love me.

I haven't always been respectful to them. Forgive me for that. I haven't always trusted in their wisdom. In fact, sometimes I found their instructions foolish. But as I mature, I realize that they give good advice. I will take what I have learned from them and put it to good use.

Now that I'm a young adult, I'm beginning to see my parents differently. Our relationship is changing. I will always be their child, but we seem to have more in common as I grow in maturity.

Father, please bless my parents, and help me never to be too busy for them. When I move out on my own, give me a gentle nudge to call them and see them often. Amen.

THINK ABOUT IT:
What can you do to form an even stronger relationship with your parents?

LET'S THINK ABOUT
THIS TOGETHER

"Come now, let us think about this together,"
says the Lord. "Even though your sins are bright
red, they will be as white as snow. Even though
they are dark red, they will be like wool."
ISAIAH 1:18 NLV

Dear God, my time in prayer with You is so valuable. Especially during this busy and challenging time in my life, I need to make time to meet with You and listen for Your words in my heart. I promise that every day I will find a quiet place to be alone with You so we can talk about what's going on with me. Together, we can address my cares and concerns and celebrate my accomplishments.

God, I'm not very good at confessing my sins to You. Sometimes I don't even recognize when I sin. So, help me with that, please. I am never afraid to come to You, because I know that when I speak to You about my transgressions, You will forgive me.

My relationship with You is the most important thing in my life, and I want it to grow stronger every day. I love You, God. Thank You for being so good to me. Amen.

THINK ABOUT IT:
Do you schedule quiet time each day to meet with God in prayer?

ALONE WITH MY PHONE

*I want you to do whatever will help you serve the
Lord best, with as few distractions as possible.*
1 CORINTHIANS 7:35 NLT

Oh, Lord, I'm tethered to my smartphone all day and into
the night—texting, browsing social media sites, looking
up information, playing music, watching videos, taking
pictures. . .all of it takes time away from You.

Forgive me for allowing my phone and all that it
does to get in the way of my relationship with You.
I'm grateful for the good things I can do with my
smartphone and other devices, but the downside is
that it can be addicting, and I know that any addiction
does not honor You.

I need to unplug sometimes, Lord, but often
that's hard to do. Please help me to unplug from all
distractions so that I may more fully appreciate all the
little things You bless me with each day. Help me to
unplug so that I will hear You more clearly and serve
You with my whole self. I'd rather be alone with You,
Lord, than alone with my phone. Amen.

THINK ABOUT IT:
Are you addicted to using your smartphone? Does it
get in the way of your relationship with God?

IT'S OKAY TO SAY NO!

"Come to me, all you who are weary
and burdened, and I will give you rest."
MATTHEW 11:28 NIV

Heavenly Father, I'm tired and feeling burned-out.
This past year leading to graduation was tough. I
worked hard to get good grades and do well on tests.
There were so many decisions I had to make and some
that I wasn't prepared for. Even getting ready for my
graduation celebration was tiring because it came in
the middle of so many other last-minute things that
had to get done. It's all behind me now, Father, and I
just want to rest.

I'm fighting saying yes to things right now. I want
a season when I can just say no to everything pressing
hard on me.

Grant me a season of rest, Lord. I don't want to
become lazy and complacent by saying no. Guide me
through the length of rest that You know I need, and
then give me the desire and energy to go forward.
Thank You, God. In Jesus' name, I pray. Amen.

THINK ABOUT IT:
Do you find it difficult to say no even when you feel
God leading you to rest?

I'M FREE!

Christian brother, you were chosen to be free.
Be careful that you do not please your old
selves by sinning because you are free.
GALATIANS 5:13 NLV

I'm free from school, textbooks, and tests, free now to make my own decisions and live my own life. Thank You, God!

You created humans to be free—to make our own choices. Some of my decisions, so far, have been good, and I think they honored You. Others have been not so good. Forgive me for them, Lord. I'm still learning.

Freedom is a wonderful feeling. I can't wait to explore all that it has to offer. I want to make wise and mature choices. I know that I have to be careful that my choosing does not lead me to sin. Now more than ever, I need to remember to come to You when I face a decision. I want the paths I take to be the right ones.

As I step out into this new life, Lord, help me to use my freedom to serve You and not myself. Guide me in all my ways. Amen.

THINK ABOUT IT:
How can you serve God with your newfound freedom?

WHOA! SLOW DOWN.

Enthusiasm without knowledge is not good.
If you act too quickly, you might make a mistake.
PROVERBS 19:2 NCV

Father, I feel like racing into the future. I want to get going and get settled into my new life. But I know that rushing into things can lead to trouble. I forget that life is not a race to the end; rather, it's a persistent and steady walk with You.

Slow me down, Lord. I want to follow You instead of running ahead. I know that You have much to teach me, and I won't learn unless I remember to take this journey one step at a time and listen to You along the way. I want to become skilled at living life the way You want me to live.

Wisdom comes not all at once but through patience. So, bless me with wisdom in Your own time and in Your own way. And bless me, too, with serenity while I wait for You.

I trust You, God. I know that You have a great plan for me, but please don't allow my enthusiasm to get in the way of making Your plan happen. Amen.

THINK ABOUT IT:
Are you so eager to move on that you are rushing ahead of God?

DRIVEN BY THE DREAM

*We continually ask God to fill you with the knowledge
of his will through all the wisdom and understanding
that the Spirit gives, so that you may live a life worthy
of the Lord and please him in every way. . .being
strengthened with all power according to his
glorious might so that you may have
great endurance and patience.*
COLOSSIANS 1:9–11 NIV

Lord, You are opening new doors for me, and I feel
in my heart that I am moving forward in accordance
with Your will. You have given me a dream—a goal to
work toward, a way to serve You. Thank You for that!

Reaching the goal will take much hard work. I
understand, and I'm ready. Sometimes I will feel tired
and overwhelmed. But these feelings are normal when
a person is driven by a dream. I trust that when I am
weary, You will give me strength to go on through Your
power. And I believe, too, that You will help me to have
patience all along the way.

I think I am going in the right direction on the
road You want me to take. I promise to stay close to
You every day so I will continue on course. Bless me,
Lord, and lead me. Amen.

THINK ABOUT IT:
Do you believe you are driven by a dream that is in
sync with God's will?

GOD'S ONE AND ONLY

You made all the delicate, inner parts of my
body and knit me together in my mother's womb.
Thank you for making me so wonderfully complex!
Your workmanship is marvelous—how well I know it.
PSALM 139:13-14 NLT

Dear God, I confess that I've compared myself to others. I've measured my skills and abilities against theirs, even my appearance, and that has led me to feel unsure of myself. While I was growing up, I admired and wanted to be just like some other people. I guess it is good, Father, to admire those who live for and serve You. But I need to remember that I should not want to be *just* like them. You made me unique—Your one and only me.

Will You help me, please, to have confidence in the me that You created? I want to be the person You made me to be, imperfections and all! Guide me to identify the special skills, talents, and character traits that You gave me to serve You. Caution me against ever thinking that someone is better than or less than me.

You made me Your child—wonderful, complex, and one of a kind. I love You, God! Amen.

THINK ABOUT IT:
Are you comfortable being God's unique creation, or do you compare yourself with others?

I WANT TO SEE THE WORLD!

If I rise on the wings of the dawn, if I settle on the far side of the sea, even there your hand will guide me, your right hand will hold me fast.
PSALM 139:9–10 NIV

Father God, I'm set free from school and my old schedules and routines. Finally, I'm on my own. Your world is so big and beautiful, and I want to see it all. I come to You in prayer today asking that You provide me with the time and finances to travel.

I wonder where You will lead me. Maybe You will bless me with a job that takes me to exciting places and adventures. Perhaps there are people on the other side of the world whom You want me to meet. How can I serve You, Lord, in places far from home?

Wherever I am, I know that You will be with me. We will travel the miles together over terrain rough and smooth. Nothing will get in the way with You guiding us; and if I'm afraid, I'll take Your hand, and You will steady me.

I'm ready, Lord. Let's go! Show me Your world. Amen.

THINK ABOUT IT:
Where in the world would you like God to take you?

ON THE JOB

*In the same way, you who are younger must
accept the authority of the elders. And all of you,
dress yourselves in humility as you relate to
one another, for "God opposes the proud
but gives grace to the humble."*
1 PETER 5:5 NLT

Dear Lord, I confess to You that at work I want to be the one in control. It is difficult for me to submit to authority sometimes, and especially on the job. I don't always agree with what my boss does, and I think I would be a better leader. Forgive me, Father!

Help me to react with respect and humility, especially when I don't agree. Keep me from having a proud, know-it-all mind-set. Help me to learn from those in authority, even by their mistakes.

I want to remember that in every job, I am working for You. That means I need to present myself in ways that please You always. Bless me with patience, understanding, and forgiveness. Give me a mature attitude. Guide me to form good relationships with everyone I work with, specifically those in charge. I'm grateful for this job You've provided for me. Thank You, God! Amen.

THINK ABOUT IT:
In your thoughts, actions, and words, do you show respect for those in authority?

PAY IT FORWARD

*And do not forget to do good and to share with
others, for with such sacrifices God is pleased.*
HEBREWS 13:16 NIV

Oh, God, You are so good to me. Every day I see
how You bless me! You have given me an education
and family and friends who support me. You watch
over me wherever I go and guide me in all my ways.
Through Your Word, You bless me with wisdom and
understanding. Where would I be without You? I don't
know how people can live and be happy unless You
are in their hearts.

Father, I want to serve You. My desire is to share
my blessings. Show me the way! Guide me to lead
others to You. Encourage me in generosity, kindness,
acceptance, and caring. Provide me with unexpected
opportunities to help others in big and small ways.
Open my eyes, Lord, to the needs all around me, and
teach me how I can satisfy them.

Make me Your servant. Use me to pay forward Your
blessings. In Jesus' name, I pray. Amen.

THINK ABOUT IT:
How can you share your blessings with others?

LIVE GOD'S WAY

When he reached the place, he said to them,
"Pray for strength against temptation."
LUKE 22:40 NCV

Dear Jesus, freedom is a wonderful thing, but I am discovering that it also comes with temptations. Every day, I face the challenge of fitting in with a new group of people. Some of them live a life that wouldn't please You, and I don't want to carelessly slip into the ways they speak, think, and act.

Even the best new opportunities come with temptations. I'm learning that there can be too much of a good thing, especially when it keeps me from spending time with You. I want my thoughts centered on You and not on the world.

You faced temptation when You walked on earth, Jesus. But You never gave in. Instead, You warned us to keep our eyes open for the evil one's traps. You told us to pray for strength against temptation.

So, Jesus, help me to stay strong. I want how I live to be a reflection of You. Amen.

THINK ABOUT IT:

If someone asked you to describe how to live a godly life, what would you say?

HIS VOICE

*If you go the wrong way—to the right or to the
left—you will hear a voice behind you saying,
"This is the right way. You should go this way."*
ISAIAH 30:21 NCV

Jesus, now more than ever, I need to listen closely for
Your voice. I am beginning a new chapter in my life,
and I have decisions to make. I believe that You will
guide me in making wise choices. Let's go someplace
quiet together. Speak gentle words to my heart. Speak
to me also when I spend time reading my Bible and
meditating on Your Word.

You said Your sheep follow You because they know
Your voice (John 10:4). I want to know Your voice, Jesus!
Teach me to discern it among all others. Provide me
with peace and assurance when the words I hear are
Yours, and give me skill and wisdom to test any inner
whispers that I am unsure of.

As I grow and mature in my relationship with You,
I will more easily recognize when it is You speaking to
me. Help me to hear You, Jesus. I want to follow You
always. Amen.

THINK ABOUT IT:
Name one way that you know it is God's voice speaking
to your heart?

WHAT IF I MESS UP?

If we confess our sins, he is faithful and just to
forgive us our sins, and to cleanse us
from all unrighteousness.
1 JOHN 1:9 KJV

Dear God, I'm human, I'm young, and I'm going to mess up sometimes. Without meaning to, and maybe even without thinking about it, I will probably do things that displease You. I'm learning about life, freedom, and independence, and, I guess, making mistakes is a normal part of that.

When I slip and fall, Father, I will come to You in prayer and confess what I did. And, like any good father, You will listen, forgive me, and remind me that there are consequences for sin. I know that You will be gentle with me because You love me and I am Yours.

Please guide me away from sin. Help me to stop and think before I do something that I know is wrong. Lead me away from peer pressure to do what I know is morally improper, and instill in me the desire to please You and have a clean heart. Amen.

THINK ABOUT IT:
After you sin, do you trust God to forgive you and continue to love you?

CREATE!

So God created humans to be like himself;
he made men and women.
GENESIS 1:27 CEV

When You made us to be like You, Lord, You gave each of us a generous helping of creativity. All of us are creative in different ways, and that's what makes life so interesting. Thank You, Father, for giving humans the ability to make things!

When I look at Your sunrises and sunsets and Your majestic mountains and verdant valleys, when I hear birds sing and see butterflies dance, I know that I have the most creative Teacher ever!

So, Father, help me to recognize what I'm good at, to refine my skills, and to use them to bring You glory. Keep me from thinking that I'm not good enough. I believe You react with joy whenever You hear me sing or when I use my mind and hands to create something good. I ask that You guide me to touch the hearts of others with the creative gifts You've given me. And God—I think You're awesome! Amen.

THINK ABOUT IT:
God gives everyone special talents. How have you used yours to honor Him?

IN THE LION'S DEN

*"My God sent his angel to shut the lions' mouths
so that they would not hurt me."*
DANIEL 6:22 NLT

Oh, heavenly Father, You are about to send me out into the world, and I'm not sure that I'm ready to go. I'm afraid.

We are living in a time of unrest, and sin seems everywhere. I worry; will something happen to hurt me? I don't want to be afraid, Father. Please calm my fears and comfort me.

I know that You are with me, and I believe that You will protect me. Nothing can happen to me outside of Your will because You have power over all evil.

Sometimes I feel like Daniel in the Bible—about to be thrown into a den of hungry lions. Will I be okay? You saved Daniel! Your angel shut the lions' mouths, and Daniel wasn't hurt. I trust You to do the same for me.

When feelings of fear overwhelm me, I will surrender them to You. And as we move forward into the world together, Lord, I will trust You to keep me safe. Amen.

THINK ABOUT IT:
Will you trust God to protect you when you take the next step in your life journey?

IT'S OKAY TO CRY

Those who cry as they carry out the seeds will
return singing and carrying bundles of grain.
PSALM 126:6 NCV

Dear Jesus, my emotions are so mixed up lately. I don't like those times when tears spill down my face for the slightest reason. This year leading to graduation was a roller coaster of ups and downs. Studying, taking tests, worrying about grades, and planning for my future—all of it made me cry. I also cried at thoughts of leaving behind my friends and what's familiar, for everything new. I'm still crying, now mostly because I'm entering the unknown. My head is filled with what-ifs.

Jesus, sometimes I get angry with myself for my tears. I think that I should show more maturity and strength. But then I remember that You cried, too (John 11:35)! So, You understand.

God did not create us to be without emotions. Thank You for reminding me of that. When my tears won't stop, Jesus, I will turn to You, and I know that You will comfort me. Amen.

THINK ABOUT IT:
How do you feel about crying? Can you think of examples in the Bible where people cried?

DETOUR?

And it will be said: "Build up, build up,
prepare the road! Remove the obstacles
out of the way of my people."
ISAIAH 57:14 NIV

Father, things are not going as I had planned. I'm not sure if You are closing doors because You want me to do something else or if these obstacles in the road are just to test my faith. Speak to me, God. What should I do?

I believe that You will remove anything that gets in the way of me following the path You want me to take. I trust You to give me the strength to break through the roadblocks, if that is what You desire. Or, maybe, there is a detour—a better route to get where You want me to be.

Here I am, Lord, quietly coming to You in prayer, seeking Your guidance. Go on ahead of me and prepare the road You want me to take. I am ready to follow You, even if it means that Your plan is different from mine. Tell me, please, which way should I go? Amen.

THINK ABOUT IT:
Have you asked God to clear the way and guide you according to His plans?

DON'T SWEAT THE SMALL STUFF!

But the Lord said to her, "My dear Martha,
you are worried and upset over all these details!"
LUKE 10:41 NLT

Dear God, I often worry about little details. I was taught in school to pay close attention to the fine points, and that's good advice. But I also know that the devil can be in the details, if I give them too much of my attention.

I get caught up in things like what to wear to an interview, giving the right answers, networking with people who can help me. . . . All of this is important for reaching my goals, but it means nothing unless I make You the center of everything.

You are in all the details of my life, Lord! If my thoughts are always on You, then everything else will fall into place.

This is a time when my mind is cluttered with small stuff. It's easy for me to slip up and forget to put You first. Forgive me! When I do that, nudge me. Give me a little shove. Say to me, "Look! Here I am!" and I will turn my thoughts toward You. Amen.

THINK ABOUT IT:
Are you so caught up in details that you forget to put God first?

JUST BREATHE

Anyone who doesn't breathe is dead,
and faith that doesn't do anything is just as dead!
JAMES 2:26 CEV

Father God, I feel like I'm sprinting through a maze and getting nowhere. I run this way and that way. I hit a dead end. I turn around, still running, looking for a way out. I'm tired, Lord, tired of running. And I wonder: Am I running from You?

Maybe You are trying to get me to slow down, to stop for a while. Is that what You want, God? Do I need some restful time alone with You?

Quiet me. Calm me. I hear You saying to me, "Breathe. Just breathe." So, measure each breath and slow me down.

I trust that You will guide me out of this labyrinth. You know the way! Today, I will stop this frantic running. I will put all my faith in You. Bless me with the rest I need. Then, renew my strength. Together we will walk in the direction You want me to go. Thank You, Father. Amen.

THINK ABOUT IT:
When you feel caught in a labyrinth, do you take time to rest and seek God's guidance?

LISTEN, READ, WATCH, LEARN

O God, you have taught me from my earliest
childhood, and I constantly tell others
about the wonderful things you do.
PSALM 71:17 NLT

You are the best teacher, God! Your lessons are everywhere in everything. When I listen to the wise counsel of mature Christians, I learn to trust and obey You. And every chapter I read in the Bible has something to teach me. You are so good to enlighten me as I read. I see how Your people help others in their times of need, and those examples educate me in ways that I can serve You.

The miracles of Your creation teach me to respect Your greatness and to honor Your gift of life. Beauty is all around me: in a newborn's cry, the scent of pine trees, the bright colors of spring flowers. . . . Everywhere I look You have put something wonderful that motivates my creativity.

Oh, Lord, You are so great! How can anyone be blind to all that You have to offer? I want everyone to know You and learn from You. I will constantly tell others about the wonderful things You do! Amen.

THINK ABOUT IT:
Look around. What lesson from God is in what you see?

WHAT IF I CAN'T TAKE CARE OF MYSELF?

*Cast all your anxiety on him
because he cares for you.*
1 PETER 5:7 NIV

Dear God, I have been dependent on others my whole life—dependent on my parents to protect and guide me, dependent on my teachers to help me learn, dependent on my friends for companionship and support. . . . But now I am entering the season when I need to break away from relying so much on others and become independent. What if I fail? What if I can't take care of myself?

I feel embarrassed to let other people know that I'm afraid to be on my own. But, God, I know that I can share that secret with You, and You will understand.

The Bible says that I can do all things through You (Philippians 4:13). So, Father, I surrender myself to You. I trust You to help with each new task I face. And if I think I can't care for myself, I will believe that I can because You care for me. Amen.

THINK ABOUT IT:

Can you think of three things you can rely on when you live on your own?

WHAT IF I DON'T LIKE IT THERE?

*And we know that all things work together for good
to them that love God, to them who are the
called according to his purpose.*
ROMANS 8:28 KJV

Lord, I'm still new at independent decision-making, and I don't solidly trust in my judgment. I think I have a good plan in place for this next big step in my life, but what if I've made the wrong choice? What if I don't like where I've chosen to go?

I guess these feelings are normal for most recent graduates. We wonder if we're taking the path that will make us happy and lead to reaching our goals. We hope that we will like our new jobs or new schools. But I want to remember, God, that You are the one who directs my steps to wherever You want me to be.

If I don't feel comfortable in my new place, I will rely on You and ask for Your guidance. I know that You will work it all out for my good as long as I trust in You. Lead me into the future, Lord. I'm ready. Amen.

THINK ABOUT IT:
How can Romans 8:28 help with your decision-making skills?

TASTE AND SEE

Taste and see that the LORD is good.
PSALM 34:8 NLT

Father God, I'm excited about all the new things that I'm about to encounter. I can't wait to try them out: new people to meet, new places to go, adventures, learning to be on my own, doing whatever I want without asking permission. Finally, I get to experience all that life has to offer!

But I know, Father, that I have to be careful. I want to taste life, but only in ways that please You. I don't want to enter into anything that will lead me astray. So, help me, please, to keep my eyes open for bad things that might be disguised as good.

As I test new experiences and relationships, help me to see them through Your eyes. Show me life the way that You want me to see it, and then lead me to react in a godly way. In everything, Lord, I will keep my thoughts centered on You and do my best to please You. Amen.

THINK ABOUT IT:

What new experiences are you looking forward to?

WOLVES DISGUISED AS SHEEP

Beware of false prophets, which come to you
in sheep's clothing, but inwardly they
are ravening wolves.
MATTHEW 7:15 KJV

Dear Lord, we live in a time when the words of Isaiah 5:20 (CEV) ring true: "You are headed for trouble! You say wrong is right, darkness is light, and bitter is sweet."

I come to You in prayer today, asking that You help me to discern right from wrong so I can separate the evil one's darkness from Your heavenly light.

I'm entering a season in my life when I will be with new people. Some may try to sway my Christian thinking. They will use words twisted to make sin seem attractive. They might even teach that in some situations sin isn't sin at all! Jesus warned about people like these, calling them wolves in sheep's clothes.

I want to be wise about what *You* say is right and wrong. Teach me through Your Word, and let the Holy Spirit be my guide. In Jesus' name, I pray. Amen.

THINK ABOUT IT:
Are your opinions on key life issues in line with God's Word?

SO MANY QUESTIONS

Ask, and you will receive. Search, and you will find. Knock, and the door will be opened for you. Everyone who asks will receive. Everyone who searches will find. And the door will be opened for everyone who knocks.
MATTHEW 7:7–8 CEV

I have many questions, God. Questions about life, my future, living according to Your will, and why bad things happen to good people. . .so many questions.

When I pray I rarely ask You about such things. I guess I think that You won't enlighten me when I ask questions that I think of as "deep." But maybe You will give me answers! After all, Jesus said that everyone who asks will receive and those who search will find.

Your answers might not be the ones I want or expect, but I trust in Jesus' words. So, God, I will ask. I will get in the habit of asking You about many things, and I will expect You to answer. I won't be afraid to ask, because You are not only my God but also my most trusted friend. I know that You will open new doors to allow me to see life through Your eyes. Thank You, God. I love You. Amen.

THINK ABOUT IT:
You likely ask God to provide for your needs, but do you also ask Him to answer your deepest questions about life?

AWESOME GOD!

As you do not know the path of the wind, or how the body is formed in a mother's womb, so you cannot understand the work of God, the Maker of all things.
ECCLESIASTES 11:5 NIV

How do You do it, God? How do You know exactly what we need and when we need it? I've seen situations worked out in amazing and unexpected ways! People show up at the precise moment a person needs a specific kind of help. Or, maybe, someone is delayed and because of it they avoid an accident. Only You know, God, how many times a day this happens. Always, You are at work in our lives.

Together with meeting our needs, there are the remarkable works of Your hands. I look at the night sky and know that You made the stars, and only You know how many there are. Sometimes I think about the places on Earth that man has never seen—hidden, undiscovered places that remain Yours alone.

Oh, God, I could go on and on about Your awesomeness. I am so grateful for You! You made me, You love me, and You will guide every step of my life. Amen.

THINK ABOUT IT:
Do you remember to praise God when you pray?

FAME!

I was the most famous person who had ever lived in Jerusalem, and I was very wise. I got whatever I wanted and did whatever made me happy. But most of all, I enjoyed my work. Then I thought about everything I had done, including the hard work, and it was simply chasing the wind.
ECCLESIASTES 2:9–11 CEV

Father, I confess to You that I've sometimes looked at celebrities—people whose names are known all over the world—and I wanted what they have. I thought about how great it would be to live knowing that I could have anything I wanted and how good it would be not to have to worry about anything. That is what I thought.

But then I read King Solomon's words in Ecclesiastes 2:9–11. He wrote them in his old age. Although he had been famous and had everything he ever wanted, he said it was all "chasing the wind." In the last verses of Ecclesiastes, Solomon says, "Everything you were taught can be put into a few words: Respect and obey God! This is what life is all about" (12:13 CEV).

I don't know what You have planned for me, God. Who knows but You? Maybe I will be rich and famous! But whatever happens, remind me that the most important thing is respecting and obeying You. Amen.

THINK ABOUT IT:
Is there a famous person whom you admire for living a God-centered life?

WHAT IF THEY LAUGH?

The LORD laughs at those who laugh at him,
but he gives grace to those who are not proud.
PROVERBS 3:34 NCV

Dear God, I'm usually brave about sharing my faith in You with my friends. I feel like they respect me, even when they don't share my belief in You. But I'm about to meet a whole new group of people, and in an unfamiliar setting. That, in itself, makes me nervous. I want to be accepted by my new coworkers or classmates.

What if they laugh at me when I tell them I am a Christian? If I walk away when they do things that displease You, will they make fun of me?

Your strongest followers, Noah, Paul, Jesus' disciples—even Jesus!—were laughed at and made fun of because they loved You. God, I will not hide my faith in You!

I ask that in my new workplace or school You will lead me to other Christians with whom I can become friends. And help me, please, never to be embarrassed or afraid to share my faith. Amen.

THINK ABOUT IT:
How will you respond if others mock your faith in God?

TIME FOR A CHANGE

"I the Lord do not change."
MALACHI 3:6 NIV

Dear God, everything is changing, and it's happening so fast. Just a short time ago, I was in a comfortable environment, in school with my teachers and classmates. Now I am about to go out on my own and begin a new life—You are giving me a makeover! I know that change is often good, but still, it's human of me to resist it. I guess few of us enjoy leaving what is comfortable and safe for the unknown.

Today, I feel lost. I'm not a student or a child dependent on my parents anymore, and I'm not yet into the new life that You are about to give me. I'm in limbo, God, in a state of transition.

Please provide me with peace, strength, and confidence as I move forward. I'm thankful that You never change. You are the one constant in my life and always in my heart. I will depend on You. Amen.

THINK ABOUT IT:
When you experience a big change in your life, how can faith in God help you?

STRESS AT HOME

"Believe in the Lord Jesus and you will be saved,
along with everyone in your household."
ACTS 16:31 NLT

Heavenly Father, this is a joyful time—graduation. But it is tarnished somewhat by problems within my family. You know what those problems are, and they weigh heavily on me sometimes. In my own ways, I've tried to fix things, but I know that I'm not capable of doing that. It's up to You, God, how things will work out.

Give me peace. As I move forward in life, I don't want to take these troubles with me. Your Word says that if I believe and trust in Jesus, He will save not only me but also everyone in my family. I will hold on to that promise.

I surrender my family and its troubles to You, Father. Free me from worry. Allow me to go on in life with a clear conscience knowing that You will remain with my family members always and that You are at work in their lives. Thank You, God. Amen.

THINK ABOUT IT:
If family problems are weighing you down, how will you rely on God for help?

MONEY, MONEY, MONEY!

The wise see danger ahead and avoid it,
but fools keep going and get into trouble.
PROVERBS 27:12 NCV

Dear God, there are many things that I want, and those things cost money. Now more than ever, I have to be wise about my spending.

Will You help me to avoid the temptation of spending more than I have? The desire to charge something and pay later is a trap that I might fall into. It's an attractive idea to have what I want right now instead of waiting until I can afford it. So, lead me away from the danger of getting into debt.

Keep me focused, please, on the best ways to spend and save. Help me to stick to my budget and not be persuaded by others to squander my money foolishly.

Father, I want to remember that every paycheck comes from You. What I earn is Your gift to me, provided to meet my needs. I want every penny that I spend and save to honor You. Amen.

THINK ABOUT IT:
Do you honor God's gift of money by the ways that you spend and save?

I AM NOT INVINCIBLE

Do you not know that your body is a house of God
where the Holy Spirit lives? God gave you His Holy
Spirit. Now you belong to God. You do not belong
to yourselves. God bought you with a great price.
So honor God with your body. You belong to Him.
1 CORINTHIANS 6:19–20 NLV

Lord, I'm young and active, and sometimes I think that nothing can stop me. When I get busy, I don't eat the way I should. Healthy choices aren't on my mind as much as grabbing a quick snack on the way to whatever I have to do. I don't get as much sleep as I should, either, or enough exercise.

I hadn't worried about this much, but when I read 1 Corinthians 6:19–20, You reminded me that my body is also where You live. I need to remember that and make caring for my body a priority.

You made my body, God. Everything that I am able to do with it is because of You. Good health is a gift, and I am not invincible. If I don't take care of myself, it might lead to illness or injury.

Father, forgive me for not always honoring You by making healthy choices. I will do my best to make my body a home fit for Your Holy Spirit. Amen.

THINK ABOUT IT:
What unhealthy habits could you change to do a better job of honoring God with your body?

INTIMACY

God wants you to be holy and to stay away from
sexual sins. He wants each of you to learn to control
your own body in a way that is holy and honorable.
1 THESSALONIANS 4:3-4 NCV

Heavenly Father, help me to stay pure in my thoughts and actions.

Movies, television, and books all provide a casual view of intimacy among young people. Society says it's okay. But I know that is not in line with Your will. Your Word says to run away from sexual sin (1 Corinthians 6:18). I want to remember that, God, and to honor You in all my intimate relationships.

Maybe Your plan for me includes marriage and a family. If so, I believe that You have already chosen my life partner. Maybe that person is someone I am with today, or maybe not. You know for sure. I don't want to be too quick to give my whole self away. I want to control my desires about intimacy and act in a way that not only honors You but also honors the person I am with. Help me, Lord, to stay strong and do what is holy and honorable in Your sight. Amen.

THINK ABOUT IT:

Do you think that your beliefs about intimacy are in line with God's will? Why or why not?

MAKING A DIFFERENCE

God brings down rulers and turns them into nothing.
ISAIAH 40:23 CEV

Dear God, the world seems to be in such a mess. In some countries, people suffer under leaders that have turned against them. Hunger and homelessness are everywhere. Sick people can't get the help they need. Everywhere I look there's trouble.

Father, I know that You are in control. You have power over all world leaders. You see what they do and measure their decisions. You give them free will to make choices, and I believe that You will punish those who use their free will to harm others.

I can't change the world, Lord, but maybe I can make a difference to help the oppressed and provide what they need. Where should I start? It all feels so overwhelming! Show me, Father, what I can do to help. Provide me with a mission, and then give me the faith, endurance, and ability to carry it out. Here I am, Lord. I'm ready. Use me. Amen.

THINK ABOUT IT:
In what small ways can you help change the world?

ONE MORE TEST!

Let us examine our ways and test them,
and let us return to the LORD.
LAMENTATIONS 3:40 NIV

Lord, before I make this next big step into life, will You test me to make sure I am becoming the person You want me to be? Am I living in a way that pleases You?

Test my people skills. Am I doing for others as I wish they would do for me? Have I chosen wisely those people whom I am closest to? Have I been forgiving and generous?

Check my speech, Lord. Am I ever careless when using Your name? Have my words hurt others or brought them down? Do I lie?

Examine my relationship with You. Have I done my best to honor You in everything I do? Have I spent time with You every day in prayer and made You the center of my life? Am I thankful enough, and do I remember to praise You?

I want to take all that I've learned from Your Word and put it into practice. So, test me. Then guide me to live a better life for You. Amen.

THINK ABOUT IT:
Have you taken a personal inventory recently to see if you are living to honor God?

WHAT IF I DON'T HAVE A PLAN?

Let me hear Your loving-kindness in the morning,
for I trust in You. Teach me the way I should
go for I lift up my soul to You.
PSALM 143:8 NLV

Father, here I am—a graduate without a plan. Everyone else seems on their way into their future. But I don't know what I should do; I need Your help.

There are many different ways that I could go, but none of them seem perfectly right. Maybe that is the problem. I want what I do to be perfect. But I know that nothing can be perfect, except You. You take everything and make it perfect in Your own way.

I have a few things that I am really good at, but I don't know where they could fit into a lifelong career. I feel lost. Show me Your kindness, God, and set a goal inside my heart, something that I can begin working toward. Give me a passionate desire to do something. Bring people into my life to inspire and lead me.

Father, I am putting all my faith and trust in You. Help me to make a plan. Teach me the way I should go. Amen.

THINK ABOUT IT:
Do you trust that God has a plan for you and that He will lead you through it?

EYES STRAIGHT AHEAD

Let your eyes look straight ahead;
fix your gaze directly before you.
PROVERBS 4:25 NIV

Oh, Jesus, I am so easily distracted. I have much to do; but I allow other things to get in the way, and I procrastinate. My phone, social media, dates with friends, movies, favorite television shows. . .I confess that I've often prioritized them over my work. I'd rather relax and have fun.

You were tempted by evil, Jesus, but You never gave in. I want to be like You. I want my relationship with God to be my first priority. I want to keep my eyes looking straight ahead and follow where He leads. My heavenly Father has given me goals and a future, and I want to honor His gift by staying focused on the path He has set for me.

Jesus, help me. Provide me with Your kind of strength—the kind that does not give in to temptation. I need to get to work. Amen.

THINK ABOUT IT:
What are some things you can do to stay focused on working toward your goals?

MEDIA SWAY

*Trust in the LORD with all your heart
and lean not on your own understanding.*
PROVERBS 3:5 NIV

Father, I'm troubled by much of what I read, hear, and see in the news. Conflicting information leaves me feeling frustrated and confused. Sometimes I can't decide which side is the right side—the one most in agreement with Your teaching.

Some of my Christian friends are quick to protest when they hear certain news stories. But they base their opinions solely on what the reports tell them. As I take this next step into adulthood, I want the truth as You know it so I can make up my mind and react in ways that honor You. I want to follow current events and stand up against whatever displeases You.

Proverbs 3:5 teaches that I should not rely too much on my own understanding. So, Lord, remind me to test my thinking by relying not only on media reports but also on scripture, prayer, and trust in You. Amen.

THINK ABOUT IT:
How do you react to media reports? Do you dig deeper for the truth?

SOUL MATES

"You should act toward the stranger who lives among you as you would toward one born among you. Love him as you love yourself. For you were strangers in the land of Egypt. I am the Lord your God."
LEVITICUS 19:34 NLV

Dear God, I'm curious about the new friends I will make as I begin this chapter of my life. It is a mystery to me. These people are strangers now, but You already know who they are, how we will meet, and what will bond us together.

You created each of us to be unique, and that is what makes friendship so interesting. I ask that You bring me Christian friends from all over the world, every ethnicity and culture. I want friends with diverse backgrounds, friends with experiences different from mine, and friends who challenge me to become an even better and more faithful Christian.

Create friendships for me that become stronger with each passing year, friendships like David and Jonathan's. The Bible says that their souls were knit together (1 Samuel 18:1 KJV). I want friends like that— soul mates!

Lord, thank You for friendship! Bless me with strangers who will soon become friends. Amen.

THINK ABOUT IT:
What can you learn from Christian friends with diverse backgrounds and experiences?

EYE TROUBLE (JUDGING OTHERS)

"You hypocrite, first take the plank out of your own eye, and then you will see clearly to remove the speck from your brother's eye."
MATTHEW 7:5 NIV

Oh, Father, I recognize that I am sometimes critical. I don't mean to be judgmental, but I am. In my thoughts and words, I condemn others. I make it known that I don't approve of their actions and how they choose to live their lives. I justify my criticism by thinking, *God would agree with me. What they do is wrong.* Even if You do agree, God, it is not my place to judge. That is up to You.

Instead of criticizing their sin, my job is to be responsible and accountable for my own sinfulness. So, Father, I confess to You that I am a sinner—just like everyone else!

Help me to be more aware of my disparaging thoughts and words. Guide me away from them so they won't take root and grow even stronger. Forgive me for judging others, Lord. Show me how to build them up instead of tear them down. Amen.

THINK ABOUT IT:
How frequently does criticism slip into your thoughts and words?

THE PRAYERS OF DAVID

O Lord God of all, hear my prayer.
Listen, O God of Jacob.
PSALM 84:8 NLV

When I can't find the words to pray, God, I can rely on prayers like this one from the book of Psalms:

"Please, LORD, hear my prayer and give me the understanding that comes from your word. Listen to my concerns and keep me safe, just as you have promised. If you will teach me your laws, I will praise you and sing about your promise, because all of your teachings are what they ought to be. Be ready to protect me because I have chosen to obey your laws. I am waiting for you to save me, LORD. Your Law makes me happy. Keep me alive, so I can praise you, and let me find help in your teachings. I am your servant, but I have wandered away like a lost sheep. Please come after me, because I have not forgotten your teachings" (Psalm 119:169–176 CEV).

Thank You, Lord, for hearing my prayer. Amen.

THINK ABOUT IT:
How can you incorporate psalms into your prayer time?

WORD OF GOD

All Scripture is inspired by God and is useful to teach us what is true and to make us realize what is wrong in our lives. It corrects us when we are wrong and teaches us to do what is right.
2 TIMOTHY 3:16 NLT

Heavenly Father, I believe it's important to know what's in the Bible. I haven't always been in the habit of reading and memorizing scripture. I'm sorry about that. It's something I want to change.

As I become more independent, I will need to handle my own problems. The best way to do that is to rely on what You say in the Bible—Your perfect guide to life. Scripture will help me to examine my heart to see if I am living according to Your teachings. It will guide me to tell the difference between right and wrong. The Bible holds words to comfort me when I am sad or lonely. It will pull me nearer to You and remind me of how much You love me.

Father, I will set aside time every day to read and meditate on Your Word. As I study Your teachings, make the meaning clear to me. Help me to apply what I learn to my life so that in every way I can honor You. Amen.

THINK ABOUT IT:
In what ways will you rely on the Bible as you enter this postgraduation phase of your life?

WHAT IF I DON'T WANT TO GET MARRIED?

*I wish that all of you were as I am. But each of
you has your own gift from God; one has
this gift, another has that.*
1 CORINTHIANS 7:7 NIV

Dear God, many of my friends are looking forward to marriage in their future. I feel differently. Right now, I don't see myself ever getting married, and I'm okay with that. Your plan for me might change, but I think You are leading me to stay single.

I'm content, Father, being on my own. It gives me more freedom to follow wherever You lead. I can spend extra time, without distractions, becoming closer to and learning from You.

Paul said that he wished his friends were single, like he was. He must have been satisfied with his single life too! But Paul also recognized that God puts in some people's hearts the desire to marry, and to others He gives the desire to stay single. Both are His gifts.

So, thank You, Father, for this gift of singleness. Show me how to use it wisely to serve You. In Jesus' name, I pray. Amen.

THINK ABOUT IT:
Which way do you feel God leading you—toward marriage or remaining single? Do you view both options as His gift?

PRAYING FOR A LIFE PARTNER

Then the LORD God said, "It is not good for the man to be alone. I will make a helper who is right for him."
GENESIS 2:18 NCV

Father God, please help me to be wise about choosing a life partner. I want the person I marry to be someone You have chosen for me.

Marriage is a major choice, and I want to choose right. Most important is that the person I say yes to is someone who loves You. I also want someone who is gentle yet strong in spirit, caring, humble, and always faithful.

Love is such a powerful feeling, so powerful that it might muddy my thinking. Give my thoughts clarity so I can identify the love that comes from You and is set apart for me and my future spouse.

Lord, I claim the promise You made in Genesis 2:18. I ask You to provide me with a life partner. Remove any obstacles in my way. You know the longings of my heart, and You know what is best for me. I commit my future into Your hands. Amen.

THINK ABOUT IT:
What do you believe are the right reasons to get married?

SOMEONE LIKE PAUL

From Paul, a servant of God and an apostle of Jesus Christ. I was sent to help the faith of God's chosen people and to help them know the truth that shows people how to serve God.

TITUS 1:1 NCV

Dear Lord, as I move on I am leaving behind people who have helped me to grow as a Christian. Distance will separate us now, and although they are with me in spirit, I will miss the everyday example they set that helped me to know You better.

In my new place, I need Christian mentors—people like the apostle Paul. He was, perhaps, the best faith booster ever! He lived to help strengthen people's faith, to teach them biblical truth, and to show them how to serve You. I want people like Paul in my life.

I am young, and I have much to learn about You and this life You have given me. I hope that someday, like Paul, I will be a mature and wise Christian who is ready to teach others. But for now, Lord, I need teachers. Will You lead them to me, please? Amen.

THINK ABOUT IT:
What qualities do you look for in a Christian mentor?

THE BEST TEACHER

"You call Me Teacher and Lord.
You are right because that is what I am."
JOHN 13:13 NLV

Jesus, there is so much to learn from You! As I read the Gospels, You reveal more and more of Yourself to me. You were always loving and compassionate, pure and holy. You were gentle, patient, and quick to forgive. You served God above everything else, and You were committed to lead others to Him. Your example of self-control cannot be matched. And You were prayerful, always making time to talk with Your Father. Oh, Jesus, You were so wise! Every word You spoke was carefully chosen and meant to encourage and teach.

I want to be more like You. Be my Teacher! Show me Your ways. Make me like Your disciples, and guide me to the truth. Build me up in wisdom and faith, and help me to be courageous when I am faced with adversity. Lead me deeper into God's Word and educate me through scripture. Thank You, Jesus! Amen.

THINK ABOUT IT:
Can you think of several ways that Jesus taught His followers to live a godly life?

ROOMMATES

God loves you and has chosen you as his own special people. So be gentle, kind, humble, meek, and patient. Put up with each other, and forgive anyone who does you wrong, just as Christ has forgiven you.
COLOSSIANS 3:12–13 CEV

Father, I wonder: What would I be like as a roommate to someone other than my family members? Would I be easy to live with or difficult? I need to think about that!

Living with someone means compromising. Am I willing to give up some of what I want? Being roommates means sharing space and putting up with each other. That might be difficult at times. Do I have patience to live with someone and accept our differences? Am I a good communicator? Would I be the kind of roommate who is responsible, trustworthy, respectful, and considerate? Do I have the people skills to know how to resolve a conflict? These are all questions I wonder about.

The idea of living with someone outside of my family is new and a little scary. So, God, help me to examine my strengths and weaknesses. Show me my real self and what I need to work on. Amen.

THINK ABOUT IT:
How might having a roommate help you to become a better person and a better Christian?

WHAT'S HOLDING ME BACK?

*Your heart should be holy and set apart for the Lord
God. Always be ready to tell everyone who asks
you why you believe as you do. Be gentle
as you speak and show respect.*
1 PETER 3:15 NLV

I'm disappointed with myself, Jesus. I'm shy about
sharing the good news that You are my Savior. I'm
not certain what holds me back from telling others
about You. I'm not embarrassed to share You! I hope
You know that. I guess I'm afraid that others will
make fun of me. And if they made fun of me, Jesus,
why would that bother me? People made fun of You,
and that didn't stop You from telling them the truth
about God.

Unless someone asks, I feel awkward talking about
my faith and everything it means to me. I don't know
what to say or when to say it.

I would like You to do this for me: Bring someone
into my life who talks openly about their faith. Help
me to learn from that person. I want to tell others why
I believe as I do. Will You help me? Amen.

THINK ABOUT IT:
What holds you back from sharing the good news
about Jesus?

I WAS WRONG

*Therefore confess your sins to each other and pray
for each other so that you may be healed. The prayer
of a righteous person is powerful and effective.*
JAMES 5:16 NIV

Dear heavenly Father, hear my prayer. I admit it; I was wrong. I felt so sure of myself when I made the mistake. When I look back at it now, I see that I reacted toward others in an arrogant and self-important way. Father, forgive me. I'm sorry.

I know that You expect me to confess my wrongdoing to those who challenged me. They gently pointed out my error, but I said that I was right. Admitting my sin to others is hard for me. Pride gets in my way. I need Your help with that. I don't want to be like the Pharisees in the Bible, self-righteous men who insisted that their thoughts and opinions were just and true.

Guide me away from always thinking that I am right. Help me, please, to humble myself. Give me strength to overpower pride, admit my mistake, and ask for forgiveness. Amen.

THINK ABOUT IT:
When you are wrong, are you quick to confess and ask forgiveness?

WHAT CAN I DO FOR YOU?

*"You must honor the Lord and truly serve
him with all your heart. Remember the
wonderful things he did for you!"*
1 SAMUEL 12:24 NCV

Oh, Lord! You have been so good to me. Thank You for the gift of life and for guiding me through each day. I'm grateful for family, friends, and teachers who have helped me along the way. You've given me everything I've needed to reach this goal in my life—graduation! Thank You!

Now, Lord, what can I do for You?

As I've read my Bible, I learned that often You call young people to carry out Your plans. Jeremiah, Samuel, David, Joseph, Ruth, Esther, and, of course, Mary, mother of Jesus—all were young, like me. So, use me!

Show me how I can serve You. Guide me to those in need and provide me with the best tools and ideas to help them. Direct me in ways I can minister to others and lead them to You. Give me all the strength and abilities I need to be of service. Use me, Lord! I'm ready. Allow me to serve You. Amen.

THINK ABOUT IT:
In what ways can you serve God?

DIPLOMA DEPRESSION

*Be happy in the Lord. And He will give
you the desires of your heart.*
PSALM 37:4 NLV

Almighty God, I have my diploma, and now I need a job. I've been applying for work, but there is so much competition, and so far, no one is interested in hiring me. I just want to get on with my life and be settled. I'm depressed over not having a job. I feel like giving up, but I know I have no choice but to keep trying. I have to support myself. I'm ready to move on.

I need You to lift me up from these feelings of despair. I believe that You hear my prayers, and I trust You to lead me. Maybe, instead of a direct path to the job I want, You've planned for me to take a detour. Show me what to do. Open doors for me.

Father, I will do my best to be happy and patient while I wait. All my faith and trust is in You. Amen.

THINK ABOUT IT:
What does it mean to be happy in the Lord?

"KEEPING" THE EARTH

And the LORD God took the man, and put him into
the garden of Eden to dress it and to keep it.
GENESIS 2:15 KJV

Dear God, thank You for the earth, my home. Thank You for its fruits, flowers, fields, and grass. I praise You for the vast variety of animals and plants, for towering mountains, rushing waterfalls, and gently flowing rivers.

Everywhere I go, Lord, there You are! You awaken all my senses to Earth's beauty. I find You in the silence of nature, in the whisper of wind through trees, in evening twilight and morning dawn. I sense Your presence in the salty scent of the ocean and in the sound of a gentle rain.

Instill in me deep reverence and respect for how Earth sustains us. Remind me of my responsibility to care for and protect it.

Bless the earth, Father God. Bless the gardeners and farmers who work the land. Bless all who strive to keep Your creation in its glory for Your honor. In Jesus' name, I pray. Amen.

THINK ABOUT IT:
In what ways are you "dressing and keeping" the earth?

IN-BETWEEN

*Forget what happened long ago! Don't think about
the past. I am creating something new.
There it is! Do you see it?*
ISAIAH 43:18–19 CEV

I'm in a state of in-between, God. I've graduated from
school, but I'm not yet into the next phase of my life.
I'm in-between youth and the maturity that comes with
age and experience. I'm in-between my old, familiar self
and the new person I am about to become. Wherever
I am, I feel. . .in-between.

At times, I wish I could rewind a few months and
go back to school where most things were predictable.
I was comfortable there. But now You have me in this
unsettled place where I'm not here nor there!

Where are You leading me? How soon will I get
there? What can I learn from You while I'm in this
limbo? Tell me, God. I'm listening.

I feel stuck but not alone. I know You are in this
place with me. So, if You are ready, let's go! I'm eager
to move on. Amen.

THINK ABOUT IT:
How can God help you grow during times of transition?

LET THEM SEE YOU IN ME

[Jesus] gave himself to rescue us from everything
that is evil and to make our hearts pure. He wanted
us to be his own people and to be eager to do right.
Teach these things, as you use your full authority
to encourage and correct people. Make sure
you earn everyone's respect.
TITUS 2:14–15 CEV

Dear Jesus, wherever You went, You taught people how to live. They learned from You, not only through Your words, but also through Your actions. You were fearless and steady, strong yet gentle. Always ready to listen, You showed compassion and sensitivity to others' needs. Even when You felt tired, You gave generously of Your time. You accepted others and showed no favoritism. Kids were welcome around You! You set an example of humility, giving credit to Your Father in heaven, obeying Him always—even when it meant pain, suffering, and death to Your body.

I want to be more like You, Jesus. In this new chapter in my life, I pray that others will see You in me. So, be my Teacher. Make me pure, gentle, faithful, and strong. Lead me to become a Christ-like example for everyone I meet. Teach me to teach others about You through my words, actions, and good works. Amen.

THINK ABOUT IT:
Today, have you set a Christ-like example? What can you do tomorrow to be more like Him?

SOCIAL MEDIA

*"You are worthy, our Lord and God, to receive glory
and honor and power, for you created all things,
and by your will they were created
and have their being."*
REVELATION 4:11 NIV

Heavenly Father, I live in a time of rapidly changing technology. My parents and teachers warned me that the internet could pull me away from You and expose me to danger. But I also discovered that the internet can be a place of learning. Through trusted websites, I've learned much about the world.

I don't want to use the internet and social media aimlessly. I believe, Father, that I can utilize them to find out more about You and also to share what I learn.

You provided Noah and others with instructions for using technology to serve You in their times. Now, will You instruct me? Lead me to websites, blogs, and articles where I can learn more truth about You. Show me how to use social media to connect with other young adult Christians sincere in their faith. When I am engaging in social media, Father, I promise to do my best to set a Christ-like example through what I post and how I interact with others. Amen.

THINK ABOUT IT:

Do you think the way you use social media is pleasing to God?

ADVENTURE AND EXPLORATION

*"Have you explored the springs from which the
seas come? Have you explored their depths?"*
JOB 38:16 NLT

I'm ready for adventures, God. I want to see the world
and explore new places. As I travel, I want to meet
interesting people and learn about their cultures.
Where will You take me?

You have instilled within me a desire to explore. So,
lead me into the depths of Your creation, and guide me
onto roads less traveled. Reveal Yourself to me along
the way. Keep me safe from danger yet unafraid to try
new things. Always remind me to stop, rest, and just
marvel at the greatness of Your work.

Life is filled with Your little surprises. Unlock all
my senses to reveal Your hidden gifts. God, show me
plants, animals, and other living things that I've never
seen, and leave me with a few mysteries to solve.

Walk with me. Establish my steps. Bless me with
joyful adventures that I will remember for the rest of
my life. Amen.

THINK ABOUT IT:
Is there someplace you have never been where you
would like to explore?

FAILING WITH GRACE

*And he said unto me, My grace is sufficient for
thee: for my strength is made perfect in weakness.
Most gladly therefore will I rather glory
in my infirmities, that the power of
Christ may rest upon me.*
2 CORINTHIANS 12:9 KJV

My friends say that I'm too hard on myself, God. But
am I? In everything, I try to do my best. Still, I rarely
live up to my expectations. Sometimes I fail, and that
bothers me. I don't like knowing that maybe I could
have done better if only I had worked a little harder. If
only. . . God, those if-onlys get me into trouble because
they take my focus away from You.

The Bible says that Your grace is sufficient for
me. Whenever I fail, You grant me Your grace. To You,
failure isn't a weakness; it's an opportunity.

Father, please help me not only to accept Your
grace, but also to extend grace to myself. Remind me
that my weaknesses are there so I might see Your
power at work within me. You don't ask that I be perfect.
Instead, You provide me with the desire to try, and then
You ask me to trust You with the result. Thank You,
God, for opening my eyes to grace. Amen.

THINK ABOUT IT:
Are you too hard on yourself, or do you offer yourself
grace when you fail?

WHAT IS A CHRISTIAN?

Guide me in your truth and teach me, for you are God my Savior, and my hope is in you all day long.
PSALM 25:5 NIV

Dear Jesus, I pray that as I go forward in my life, You will teach me what it really means to be a Christian.

I know that a Christian is someone who has accepted You as their Lord and Savior. A Christian is forgiven for their sins and has a home ready in heaven when they die. But Christianity is so much more than that! It is about love—Yours for us and ours for You. It is about unselfish service to others. And it is about learning what it means to embrace the Christian faith and follow You.

Teach me, Jesus! Teach me as Your disciple. Show me how to live each day with You leading me. I want to follow You wholeheartedly and submit to You, even when it's hard. And I want to share what I learn. Provide me with the words and the way to lead others to You.

Thank You, Jesus, for being my Lord and Savior. Amen.

THINK ABOUT IT:
What do you think it means to be a Christian?

I'M STRUGGLING

Don't worry about anything, but pray about everything.
With thankful hearts offer up your prayers and requests
to God. Then, because you belong to Christ Jesus,
God will bless you with peace that no one can
completely understand. And this peace will
control the way you think and feel.
PHILIPPIANS 4:6–7 CEV

Heavenly Father, I'm struggling. This should be a happy time, but instead I feel anxious about this next big step in my life. I'm worried and even afraid, and I don't like feeling this way.

Everyone is congratulating me on graduating and asking me what I plan to do with my life. It's overwhelming because I'm not sure what I want to do next. I have a plan, but I'm not certain that it's the best one. I'm wrestling with myself trying to decide which way to go, and I'm never at peace.

Will You help me, God? I really need You. I need some of that peace that no one can completely understand. I submit all my anxiety and fear to You, Father. Take it away from me, please, and allow Your peace and love for me to control the way I think and feel. Thank You, God. Amen.

THINK ABOUT IT:
Can you think of a time when you were anxious and God provided someone or something that brought you peace?

PRIDE

*Nothing should be done because
of pride or thinking about yourself.*
PHILIPPIANS 2:3 NLV

Father, forgive me. I've let pride get in my way. When I received my diploma, I believed that it was a symbol of entitlement. I thought it meant that I was owed a good job with a great salary and benefits. I viewed it as a ticket to realize all my hopes and dreams. But, God—then I thought that I wouldn't have that diploma if it weren't for You! You are the one who has brought me this far, and You will lead me into the future.

When I hadn't received what I hoped for, I thought: *I deserve more. I deserve better!* But then, God, I remembered that You give me exactly what I need.

I'm sorry for allowing pride to get between You and me. I'm grateful to You for my education. I'm grateful to You for this milestone—graduation. Now, Lord, as You lead me ahead, I ask You to bless me with an attitude of humility. All I have and all I am is only because of You. Amen.

THINK ABOUT IT:
Does pride get in your way, or do you give God credit for everything you accomplish?

"COME AND TALK WITH ME."

My heart has heard you say, "Come and talk with me."
And my heart responds, "LORD, I am coming."
PSALM 27:8 NLT

I hear You, God! You want me to come talk with You.
I'm coming. Here I am!

I've thought of prayer as being a formal kind of
conversation, but You have taught me that I should come
to You just as I am: respectful always in my conversations
with You, but not guarded. You know everything about
me, so I shouldn't hold back. I can talk with You like I
would a trusted friend—because that is what You are,
my best friend!

God, sometimes I forget that I can talk with You
all day long. You are always with me, so why shouldn't
we talk? Please speak through my heart, and open my
ears to hear You. Wherever I am, I can converse with
You silently.

I'm so grateful for Your friendship. It brings me joy,
comfort, and peace. And wisdom, God! Your wisdom
guides me every day. Oh, thank You for talking with
me. Thank You for being my friend. Amen.

THINK ABOUT IT:
How often do you have conversations with God?

FOLLOW THE LEADER

*We ask you, Christian brothers, to respect those who
work among you. The Lord has placed them over you
and they are your teachers. You must think much
of them and love them because of their work.
Live in peace with each other.*
1 THESSALONIANS 5:12–13 NLV

Father God, as I enter this new season of work and
service, please give me a right attitude toward my
coworkers and those I work for. Encourage me to be
respectful always, and especially when I disagree.

I know, Lord, that You place me exactly where
You want me. You set me among people who have
something to teach me. Their lessons might be about
my work, or their purpose might be to help me grow
as a Christian. Remind me of that, particularly when
relationships turn difficult.

Help me to see the good in people and to be a
source of encouragement and strength. Guide me to
build people up instead of tear them down, and lead
me to love them the way that You do.

Father, I want to follow Jesus' example and bring
peace into all my relationships at work and elsewhere.
Show me how to do that. In His name, I pray. Amen.

THINK ABOUT IT:
What can you do to have peaceful relationships with
those you work with and for?

I'M RESPONSIBLE

Each person must be responsible for himself.
GALATIANS 6:5 NCV

This is all new to me, God, this freedom of being totally responsible for myself. I like the idea of it, but in some ways, I feel a little bit lost. I'm used to having my parents and others set rules and boundaries for me. But now, I'm responsible for setting my own.

I want to experience life, but I don't want to go so wild with freedom that I lose sight of You and how You want me to live. I want to be mature in how I handle myself, and I want to please You.

Guide me to make a set of rules for myself, rules that will keep me aligned with Your will. Give me courage to follow those rules and not give in to peer pressure. Lead me into adulthood, God. Teach me to be wise with my choices, and help me to become the person You want me to be. Amen.

THINK ABOUT IT:
Have you set rules and boundaries for yourself?

HONOR THE LORD

Honor the LORD with your wealth and with
the best part of everything you produce.
PROVERBS 3:9 NLT

Oh, Jesus, You have been so good to me. I want to honor You for all You have done.

I will remember what the Bible says: "What can I offer the LORD for all he has done for me? I will lift up the cup of salvation and praise the LORD's name for saving me. I will keep my promises to the LORD in the presence of all his people" (Psalm 116:12–14 NLT). Jesus, I will readily tell others about Your gift of salvation, and I will do my best to keep all the promises I make to You. I will read and live by Your Word. I will honor You through tithing; and with every good thing I do, I will give the praise and glory to You. I will worship You through my words and my actions all the days of my life and be grateful to You for all that You have done. Amen.

THINK ABOUT IT:
What can you do to thank Jesus for all He has done for you?

THE GIFT OF ENCOURAGEMENT

*And let us consider how we may spur one
another on toward love and good deeds.*
HEBREWS 10:24 NIV

Dear God, I come to You today asking for a gift: please provide me with the ability to encourage others.

I want to be the sort of person who makes others aspire to love and serve You. I want to lift them up when they are down and challenge them to be all that they can be by trusting in You. I desire to offer practical help and remind them of Your promises.

Lord, I aim to present a positive and Christ-like example for everyone I meet. I long to show love to those who believe that they are unlovable. I hope to inspire those who live a life of sin to turn toward and serve You. I want to do what is good for all and lead them to do good for others.

Please, God, bless me with the gift of encouragement, not for my own sake, but for Yours. Amen.

THINK ABOUT IT:
Can you think of five ways to encourage others?

LIFT ME UP!

*Open my eyes to see the
-miracles in your teachings.*
PSALM 119:18 NCV

Lord, when I was a young child, my father lifted me onto his shoulders so I could view the world from his perspective. Everything looked different from there, up high. I felt safe and secure because I trusted my father not to let me fall.

In some ways, I feel like that little kid again. There's so much of the world that I haven't seen, and I'm eager to know what's out there beyond my sight.

Will You lift me up, Lord? Lift me safe onto Your shoulders. Walk with me resting there up high. Help me to see the world through Your eyes, and teach me as we go. Where will You take me? I won't be afraid, because I trust You. I know that You have a firm grasp on me, and You won't allow me to fall.

I'm ready, Lord. Let's go! Show me Your world. Amen.

THINK ABOUT IT:
Have you asked God to show you the world through His eyes?

RIGHT VS. WRONG

I have discovered this principle of life—that when I want to do what is right, I inevitably do what is wrong. I love God's law with all my heart. But there is another power within me that is at war with my mind. This power makes me a slave to the sin that is still within me.

ROMANS 7:21-23 NLT

Heavenly Father, why is it that sin sneaks up on me? When I come to You in prayer at the end of the day, I always have something to confess, even when I've tried my best to do what is right. A harsh word spoken, a wrong attitude, a lie disguised as an excuse—little things sneak in, every day, without me noticing.

Forgive me, Father. I want to do right, but as Romans 7:21-23 says, there is another power within me that is at war with my mind.

Save me from Satan's traps. Help me to be more aware of sin before I allow it to overtake me. Remind me to think before I speak, to have a positive attitude, and to be gentle and kind toward all.

I love You, God, and I want to please You; but when I don't, I thank You for Your mercy, forgiveness, and grace. Amen.

THINK ABOUT IT:
How have you sinned today—without even noticing?

GOD IS MY EVERYTHING

*You are my mighty rock, my fortress, my protector,
the rock where I am safe, my shield, my powerful
weapon, and my place of shelter.*

PSALM 18:2 CEV

Oh, God, as I take this next big step in my life, I won't worry or be afraid because You are my everything!

Father, You are my protector. You stand in front of me like a rock. Nothing can break through Your shield. You are my fortress, my safe place. You shelter me from life's storms. You prepare a quiet place for me to rest. And whatever I need, You provide it.

You go before me, checking my path, clearing any obstacles in my way. You are my guide, the One who leads me toward success and prosperity. My faith and trust are in You.

I am Your servant, Lord. You are my Master, my Teacher, and my Friend. You never leave my side. No place is foreign to You because You are everywhere. I feel secure with You, wherever I go.

Oh, thank You, God, for all that You are. Thank You for being my everything. Amen.

THINK ABOUT IT:
Can you list several roles God plays in your life?

A CLEAR CONSCIENCE

*"So I strive always to keep my
conscience clear before God and man."*
ACTS 24:16 NIV

Jesus, I've come to thank You for Your gifts of forgiveness and salvation. It comforts me knowing that although I'm a sinner, You've reserved a place for me in heaven.

I read my Bible and memorize scripture, and every day I learn more about God's character and Your teachings. I know what's expected of me. Still, I mess up and disappoint myself through my actions, words, and deeds. I do my best to live for God, and I strive to act in a way that keeps my conscience clear. But, just like everyone else, I fall short of my goal.

Jesus, please help me to become more like You. I want to do better and be better so that when I come to God in prayer, He will say to me, "You worked hard today and did your best. I'm pleased with you. Well done."

Thank You, dear Jesus. I love You. Amen.

THINK ABOUT IT:
Is something weighing on your conscience today that you need to share with God?

MY PARENTS WON'T LET GO

*Jesus said to them, "For sure, I tell you, anyone
who has left his house or parents or brothers or wife
or children because of the holy nation of God will
receive much more now. In the time to come
he will have life that lasts forever."*
LUKE 18:29-30 NLV

Dear God, I am coming to You with a problem. It's time for me to leave home, but my parents are having a hard time accepting it. Their sadness makes me sad. Even worse, it makes me less confident about leaving. I feel guilty sometimes, like leaving them is a bad thing.

I know, Father, that everyone has to leave their parents at some point. It's a part of growing up. My parents have taught me to love You, to follow Your teachings, and to trust You. So why won't they trust *me*?

I don't know what to do. I want to leave home in a respectful way that honors my parents. They have been great to me, and I don't want to hurt them. Will You help them, please, to accept this? Will You help us all to make this a smooth and joyful transition?

Thank You, Father, for hearing my prayer. Amen.

THINK ABOUT IT:
What can you do to make your leaving home easier for your parents?

BE THANKFUL ANYWAY

In everything give thanks. This is what God
wants you to do because of Christ Jesus.
1 THESSALONIANS 5:18 NLV

Father God, You gave me life and have provided for me every day. You've loved me through good times and bad, forgiven my sins, and picked me up when I was down. Throughout my life, You've stayed with me, guided me, and protected me. Your blessings are too many to count—and, so often, I forget to thank You. Please forgive me.

Your Word says that I should give thanks in everything. I've been careless about that. If I've had a bad day, I forget to thank You for another day of life. If someone disrespects me, I forget to thank You that I am able to forgive. In so many circumstances I've failed to find a reason to be thankful—and I'm sorry.

I'm grateful, Father, for good days, bad days, and every day. Thank You for joy and also for tears, for lessons that come easy and for those that challenge me.

Most of all, I'm grateful for You! God, I love You. Amen.

THINK ABOUT IT:
In every circumstance, do you find something to be grateful for?

UNABASHED CONFIDENCE

*So do not throw away your confidence; it will be
richly rewarded. You need to persevere so that
when you have done the will of God, you will
receive what he has promised.*
HEBREWS 10:35–36 NIV

Heavenly Father, I'm ready to take this next step in my
life. I'm stepping out boldly, with confidence, because
I know that You are leading me.

Whatever lies ahead, You are already there working
it out for my best and for Your glory. I can count on
that! You are my Good Shepherd, watching over me
and providing me with all that I need.

I am confident that as long as I put my trust in
You, I will be okay. I'm sure there will be difficult and
challenging times ahead, but together we'll get through
them. With confidence in the power You give me, I will
triumph over obstacles in my way.

There is no place in my heart for self-confidence,
Lord, because my heart is filled up with unabashed
God-confidence. My faith and hope are in You, and
my desire is to follow Your will and to serve You well.
In Jesus' name, I pray. Amen.

THINK ABOUT IT:
Check the source of your confidence. Is it self-
confidence or God-confidence?

IT'S TOO HEAVY

Cast thy burden upon the LORD, and he shall sustain thee: he shall never suffer the righteous to be moved.
PSALM 55:22 KJV

It's too much, Lord! Change is happening too fast, and I feel like I'm caught up in the wind. I just want to go someplace quiet and get away from it all. Will You help me, please? I need this intense feeling to go away.

Let's go somewhere quiet and talk. I need to hear Your voice, and I long for You to comfort me. I will turn my thoughts away from my troubles and allow Your love to fill me up. I'll escape this heavy load for a while and rest with You.

You promise to sustain me, and I trust that You will. I believe that if I give You this mess of feelings inside me, You will sort them out.

Hear my prayer, Lord. Stay with me. Cover me with Your gentleness and love. Give me rest, and then send me back into the world refreshed and ready to move on. Amen.

THINK ABOUT IT:
Can you think of a time when you felt overwhelmed and God sustained you?

WHEN FAITH COMES AND GOES

If we have no faith, He will still be faithful
for He cannot go against what He is.
2 TIMOTHY 2:13 NLV

Dear Jesus, I am like Your disciple Peter. When he saw You walking on the water toward his boat, he doubted it was You.

Peter said, "If it is You, Lord, tell me to come to You on the water." And You said, "Come!" Peter got out of the boat, and he walked on the water to You. But when he saw the wind, he was afraid. He began to sink. He cried out, "Lord, save me!" You reached out and held him steady. You said to Peter, "You have so little faith! Why did you doubt?" (Matthew 14:28–31 NLV).

My faith comes and goes, like Peter's. I want to be strong and believe that You will help me, but fear and doubt get in my way. Still, I know that You remain faithful to me, even when my faith wanes.

Strengthen my faith, Jesus. Help me to always trust in Your gentleness, care, and love for me. Thank You for being my Savior and my Friend. Amen.

THINK ABOUT IT:
How would you measure your faith on a scale of one to ten?

PLAN OVERLOAD

The LORD says, "My thoughts are not like your
thoughts. Your ways are not like my ways."
ISAIAH 55:8 NCV

God, is it possible for me to overplan my life? One of my strong points is that I'm conscientious about everything. I plan a schedule and stick to it. I'm always careful not to make mistakes. I work hard and do my job well. Still, things don't always work out as I expect, and often I'm stressed instead of at peace. Could it be that I'm planning too much and getting in the way of Your will for me?

I confess that my thoughts more often turn toward goals I set for myself instead of those You have for me. Forgive me for that! Maybe I need to loosen up a little and relax knowing that You are in control.

I promise, Father, to begin each day spending time with You and seeking Your guidance. I promise to let go of my rigid schedules and expectations and allow You to lead me. Help me, God, to keep these promises! My faith and trust are in You. Amen.

THINK ABOUT IT:
Is it easy or difficult for you to surrender your will to God's?

BACK TO SCHOOL

I will instruct you and teach you in the way
you should go; I will counsel you with
my loving eye on you.
PSALM 32:8 NIV

Dear God, I'm grateful to have graduated and to be finished for a while with classroom learning. But there is one classroom I will never leave—Yours!

You have taught me every day of my life, guiding me through first words and first steps, and then leading me to more difficult and challenging tasks. Each new experience held a lesson. Some I readily learned; others took time. A few I set aside and haven't returned to—yet.

I learn when You speak to me through the Bible, and I learn when You give a familiar passage fresh meaning that applies to my life exactly when I need it!

I'm grateful for Your Holy Spirit who whispers to my heart and teaches me to live in a godly way.

Continue to instruct me. Guide me steadily toward wisdom. Help me, Father, to set my focus on You and the lessons You want me to learn. Amen.

THINK ABOUT IT:
In what ways does God counsel you?

A NEW LIFE

"If you return to the Almighty,
you will be restored—so clean up your life."
JOB 22:23 NLT

Oh, Jesus. I've really messed up. I've put everything I want to do ahead of what You wanted, and it's gotten me nowhere.

I made it to graduation. That was a big step, and I only got there thanks to You. Somehow, You kept me going when I wanted to quit.

I haven't thought much about sin. In fact, it wasn't a word that I ever used to describe my behavior. But I've sinned, Jesus—I've sinned a lot! And, most of the time, I felt guilty. I knew that what I did was wrong.

The Bible says that if I return to You and confess my sin, You will restore me and allow me a fresh start. I believe in You, Jesus. I believe that You died on the cross so my sin would be forgiven. Thank You for loving me so much that You died for me!

I'm ready to clean up my act. So, Jesus, restore me and help me to live my life to please You. Amen.

THINK ABOUT IT:
Are you living a new life, or do you need to clean up your act?

PEACE

They don't know how to live in peace, and there is
no fairness in their lives. They are dishonest.
Anyone who lives as they live will
never have peace.
ISAIAH 59:8 NCV

God, why do people hate? Why is there so much division and turmoil in the world?

When I read the Bible, I see that it has always been this way. Since the garden of Eden, there has never been a time when humans lived without sin—or without fighting each other. But, God, I think it's worse during this time I live in. Weapons are more sophisticated now and powerful enough to wipe out whole countries. And leaders threaten to use them. They speak hateful words about other nations.

I know that I can't change the world, but I want to do something to help bring peace, if just in my little corner of the world. What can I do? Show me! Surely, You can use me in some way. Put me together with an army of like-minded people. Together, maybe we can make a difference. I'm ready to serve You, Father. Amen.

THINK ABOUT IT:
What can you do to bring peace into your little corner of the world?

ONE AMONG MANY

For I am persuaded, that neither death, nor life,
nor angels, nor principalities, nor powers, nor things
present, nor things to come, nor height, nor depth,
nor any other creature, shall be able to separate
us from the love of God, which is in
Christ Jesus our Lord.
ROMANS 8:38–39 KJV

Dear Lord, I'm just one of those who graduated in my class. I'm only one in a sea of graduates from all around the country. Still, You know me. You know everything about me, and best of all, You love me!

One or one hundred million—it makes no difference to You. Each of us is dear to You and loved.

The Bible tells me that You care so much about me that You know how many hairs are on my head. It also says that You see the comings and goings of each of Earth's sparrows (Matthew 10:29–30). No living thing escapes Your sight or is ever outside of Your care.

Your love is so great. It fills me up! It is there in all circumstances, powerful, forgiving, understanding, and gentle. Your love comforts me, lifts me, and encourages me! Nothing can separate me from Your love.

Although I am just one among many, You make me feel special. Oh, Father! Thank You for loving me. I love You too. Amen.

THINK ABOUT IT:
How does God show you His love?

ENCOURAGE EACH OTHER

*Therefore encourage one another and build
each other up, just as in fact you are doing.*
1 THESSALONIANS 5:11 NIV

Father, open my eyes today to those who could use some building up. Then lead me to encourage them in just the right ways.

Show me how to encourage strangers I meet. It might be something as simple as a smile when I pass someone in a parking lot. Or maybe I could exchange some friendly conversation with the person ahead of me in the checkout line. I could compliment someone on her outfit or say something kind to the guy who takes my fast-food order. Show me what to do, God!

Guide me today to encourage my family, friends, and coworkers. Make me sensitive to their needs. Remind me to be a caring listener, and give me the best words to respond to their concerns.

I want to cheer people up, give them confidence, support them, and help however I can.

So, God, direct me to be an encourager today. Allow me to see others through Your eyes. Amen.

THINK ABOUT IT:
Can you easily spot someone who needs encouragement?

FATHER OF THE FATHERLESS

If my father and mother leave me,
the LORD will take me in.
PSALM 27:10 NCV

Heavenly Father, graduation should be a happy time for all, but some graduates are unhappy because they don't have the kind of support they need from their parents. My prayer today is for every young person who has trouble at home.

Be with those who feel like they have been abandoned. Their hearts ache. Please comfort them and lift them up!

The Bible says that You are Father to the fatherless (Psalm 68:5). You help the poor and children without parents (Job 29:12). I ask, Lord, that You would open the hearts of every young person who feels uncared for. Show them that they are not alone. Take them in, and fill their hearts with Your love.

Heal suffering relationships between children and parents. Mend broken homes. Bring families together on graduation day by destroying walls of pride and unforgiveness. Allow love to overcome hate. I ask these things in Jesus' name. Amen.

THINK ABOUT IT:
What does Psalm 27:10 tell us about God's attitude toward children in broken homes?

IN EVERYTHING. . .

"So in everything, do to others what you would have them do to you, for this sums up the Law and the Prophets."
MATTHEW 7:12 NIV

Dear God, I know the Golden Rule: In everything do to others what you would have them do for you. But I'm not always good at following it. Forgive me.

Sometimes my attitude needs adjusting. I can be ill-tempered and complaining, uncooperative or sullen. I don't enjoy being with people who have unpleasant attitudes, so I know that I'm not fun to be around when my attitude is bad. I promise to work on that.

I want to get better at recognizing what I need from others. I want to be more sensitive to how I would hope to be treated when I am at my worst. That will help me to become more aware of, and empathetic toward, everyone.

Give me patience. Help me to be understanding when someone around me is having a bad day. Teach me how Jesus would treat them, and then lead me to follow His example.

Thank You, Father, for always forgiving me and loving me. Amen.

THINK ABOUT IT:
Do you need to become better at following the Golden Rule?

CODE OF CONDUCT

Only one thing concerns me: Be sure that you live in a way that brings honor to the Good News of Christ.
PHILIPPIANS 1:27 NCV

As I step into this new phase of my life, God, I want to make You proud. I want my behavior to honor You.

I'm shedding my old ways and putting on a new attitude. I'm reading the Gospels and learning about Jesus so I can act more like Him. My hope is that, in my new life, others will see Jesus through me.

Change is happening. You are reinventing me, and I'm glad. I embrace this change in me, and I don't want anything to get in the way. Please keep me from falling into Satan's traps and slipping back into my old behaviors.

Instead of following the crowd, I choose to follow You! Inspire me toward a new code of conduct. Make me aware of any words and actions that do not honor You, and then help me to change.

Father, I surrender all that I am to You. Mold me and shape me into a disciple of Christ. Amen.

THINK ABOUT IT:
How would you define a Christian code of conduct?

SOUL SEARCHING

*And thou shalt love the L*ord *thy God with all thine heart, and with all thy soul, and with all thy might.*
Deuteronomy 6:5 kjv

Father God, I've been soul searching, thinking about my relationship with You. I've decided that our relationship needs improvement. I haven't been good at making it my priority, and I'm sorry. But I'm here now, listening with my heart and doing my best to love You with all my soul and might.

I've let life get in the way, forgetting that there would be no life were it not for You. My priorities have been wrong—I've put so many things ahead of my relationship with You. I've been lazy about setting aside time just for You and me alone, and I haven't been good about reading the Bible and learning all that I can from You.

Allowing my relationship with You to slip leaves me feeling empty inside. I hate that feeling! Forgive me, God. I will try to do better. Thank You for loving me, and please help me to love You more each day. Amen.

THINK ABOUT IT:
What can you do to strengthen your relationship with God?

HONESTLY!

The Lord hates lying lips,
but those who speak the truth are His joy.
PROVERBS 12:22 NLV

Lord, how many times has the word *honestly* come from my lips when I've exaggerated? How many times have I told a little white lie or lied to spare someone's feelings?

I don't believe that You honor any form of lie, no matter how small it might be. Help me to remember the words of Proverbs 12:22—You hate lies!

A lie is a lie. If I tell someone I like their new hairstyle and I don't, that's a lie. If I say, "I'll be right there," and then show up late, that's a lie. So many lies, God! And mostly, I'm not aware of them.

Please help me not only to be aware but also to tell the truth in love. That's a difficult thing to do sometimes, but I want to learn how. I know You can teach me.

Forgive me, Father, for my lies, and guide me to always speak the truth. Amen.

THINK ABOUT IT:
Half truths, false flattery. . .can you name several other examples of lies?

LIGHT UP MY PATH

*Your word is a lamp that gives
light wherever I walk.*
PSALM 119:105 CEV

Dear God, I'm not sure what lies ahead, but I've started walking. I've taken this next step on my life journey. I'm moving tentatively, trying not to trip or fall.

I believe that the Bible will be my guide. It is my map into the future, and it holds the answers to many of my questions. I will study it every day and follow where it leads me.

God, I ask You to unlock its words and make them apply to my life. Grow my personal relationship with You through Your Word. Speak to me through scripture. I trust You to go ahead of me into the darkness. I'm counting on You to light up my path.

Wherever I go, I will take my Bible with me. It will be my constant companion now and for the rest of my life, and I will treasure its words like gold inside my heart. Amen.

THINK ABOUT IT:
Do you trust the Bible as your travel guide to the future?

WHEN TO SAY, "I CAN'T"

The righteous person faces many troubles,
but the LORD comes to the rescue each time.
PSALM 34:19 NLT

Oh, God, I have a friend who is in deep trouble and relying on me for help. I've done my best to listen and give advice. I've suggested that my friend get help from a counselor or a trusted older adult. But nothing I say or do has worked. I'm afraid for this person, Father. The problem is too big for me to solve, and I can't do this anymore.

Should I tell someone what is going on and get help for my friend? I don't want to cause more trouble, but I'm worried. Please, God, will You step in and do something?

This is a time of change for all of us graduates. We're leaving a familiar place in our lives and going into someplace new. It's really hard for some people to make the change. So, help my friend, Father. I can't carry this burden alone. Show me what to do, and then give me the courage to do it. Amen.

THINK ABOUT IT:

What would you do if a friend needed more help than you were able to provide?

TATTOOS, PIERCINGS, AND PURPLE HAIR

"The LORD does not look at the things people look at. People look at the outward appearance, but the LORD looks at the heart."
1 SAMUEL 16:7 NIV

Father, I wonder what You think when You see all the different styles people wear. I know some who have tattoos and others who would never get one. Most of my classmates had pierced ears, and a few had many piercings. And hair, God—so many styles and colors—red, purple, green, blue, curly, shaven, and straight!

All over the world, in different cultures, people wear various styles. Some wear most of their body covered and others wear few clothes. Some dress conservatively and others casual.

What do You see, God? Your Word says You don't look at the things people look at. You look at the heart. I want to do the same and not judge people by their appearance.

You give us freedom to make our own choices. Still, I want to dress in a way that honors You. So, guide me, Father, to choose my styles wisely. Amen.

THINK ABOUT IT:
What guides your personal choice in the styles you wear? Do you think you honor God by the way you dress?

IS IT OKAY TO CHANGE MY GOAL?

I don't run without a goal.
And I don't box by beating my fists in the air.
1 CORINTHIANS 9:26 CEV

Dear God, I thought I was running toward what I wanted. For a long time, I felt passionate that my plan was the right one. But now my desire to reach that goal has faded. As I try to follow my plan, I'm reminded of what Paul wrote in 1 Corinthians 9:26—it feels like I'm boxing, beating my fists in the air.

I wonder: Are You leading me to do something else? Is it You who took my passion away and made my plan lukewarm? I feel my heart pulling me in a new direction. Is that what You want? Is it okay to change my goal?

You have the answers to my questions. So, tell me what I should do. Help me to be at peace with my decision, and lead me where You want me to go. I trust You, God. Please show me the way. Amen.

THINK ABOUT IT:

Are you at peace with the goal you're working toward, or do you feel God pulling you in a different direction?

STRANGE NEW RITUALS

*I have learned to be content
whatever the circumstances.*
PHILIPPIANS 4:11 NIV

Dear Lord, everything is different now. From the time when I wake up in the morning until I go to bed at night, my life is filled with newness. I don't mind change when it comes a little at a time. But this is almost too much. Everything that was comfortable seems to be shifting to all things strange and unfamiliar.

I'm entering that season of adulthood when change happens rapidly. It's that period between school and settled, and the transition will take time.

I want to feel content as my circumstances change, and I believe that I know how. I will keep my mind fixed on You and come to You often in prayer to seek Your direction and guidance. If I put my faith and trust in Your love, then I know that I will be all right.

Here I am, Father. Please lead me into contentment. Amen.

THINK ABOUT IT:
What is the source of your contentment?

BALANCING PRIDE WITH HUMILITY

Let someone else praise you, not your own mouth—a stranger, not your own lips.
PROVERBS 27:2 NLT

Father God, I need Your guidance regarding pride. All my life, I've practiced humility. I've always been quiet about my achievements. I'm even embarrassed when my family members and teachers praise my accomplishments. But now, as I look for a job or apply to attend a new school, I'm expected to promote my good works. I struggle with that.

The Bible says in Proverbs 16:18 (NLT): "Pride goes before destruction, and haughtiness before a fall." But it also says in Ecclesiastes 3:22 (KJV): "There is nothing better, than that a man should rejoice in his own works."

Is there such a thing as good pride? I think it might be okay to talk about my good works if I remember that they are because of You. When I promote them and give You the credit, I think that is one way of showing humility.

Guide me, Father. Show me how to rejoice in my own works and still remain humble. Amen.

THINK ABOUT IT:
Is pride always a sin, or can pride be a good thing?

WHAT IF I'M BORED?

Be very careful, then, how you live—not as unwise but as wise, making the most of every opportunity, because the days are evil.
 EPHESIANS 5:15–16 NIV

Until I get settled in a career someday, Lord, I need to take whatever jobs I can find. I have to confess that sometimes I'm bored at work. I'm sorry to tell You that, Father, but it's true. Forgive me. Much of the time I wish I were someplace else.

I know that boredom isn't good for me. It allows my mind to wander, and it keeps me from doing my best on the job.

Will You help me to find something good at work, something that will motivate me and keep me from falling into boredom? I want to make the most of every opportunity You give me. I know that You have placed me in this specific job for a good reason. So, help me to get the most from it, please. I want to be content and honor You at work and in everything I do. Amen.

THINK ABOUT IT:
How can you turn boredom at work into God-honoring productivity?

EXPECTATION VS. REALITY

We all fall short of God's glorious standard.
ROMANS 3:23 NLT

Dear God, I've always expected a lot from myself and made every effort to be perfect. I've studied hard and felt disappointed in myself if I got less than an A on my school assignments and tests. I've put a lot of pressure on myself to do well, and most of the time I was successful!

But, Father, now I find myself in a place where the competition is greater. If I measure myself against others, I'm not so perfect anymore. That makes me feel depressed and not good enough. . . .

Today I remembered that the Bible says You are the only one who is perfect! I think I've put too much thought and worry into the idea of perfectionism. I need to relax my expectations a bit and accept the reality that no one is perfect. I'll still strive to do my best, Father, but I promise not to make myself crazy over it anymore.

Will You help me to accept and be content with myself, just the way I am? Amen.

THINK ABOUT IT:
Do you expect too much from yourself?

LUKEWARM FAITH

But since you are lukewarm and neither
cold nor hot, I will spit you out of my mouth.
REVELATION 3:16 CEV

Dear Jesus, the words of Revelation 3:16 are Yours. You were speaking about the church in Laodicea, and You made reference to an analogy about water. If it was cold, water was refreshing. The hot spring water was perfect for bathing in. But lukewarm water didn't have a similar value. The church was lukewarm in its faith toward You.

Jesus, sometimes I allow my faith to become lukewarm. I'm sorry. You are the most important one in my life, and I want my faith to always be on fire, burning in its desire for You. I want to remember, every minute of my life, that You died so my sins would be forgiven. You are the reason that I will have eternal life in heaven.

Thank You, Jesus! Forgive me for my lukewarm faith. I am grateful to You for all that You are and all that You have done for me. Amen.

THINK ABOUT IT:
How would you describe the temperature of your faith?

EVERY WHICH WAY BUT YOU

See to it that no one takes you captive through hollow and deceptive philosophy, which depends on human tradition and the elemental spiritual forces of this world rather than on Christ.

COLOSSIANS 2:8 NIV

Father, at school, through friendships, and even through various forms of media, I'm faced with many different philosophies about life and religion.

I've heard teachers and classmates refer to You as the Universe. Some believe in many gods, each with an individual superpower. I know people who connect You equally with nature. There are some who are agnostic, not sure of Your existence. And others have chosen atheism, not to believe in a god at all.

The world is filled with clashing philosophies, and I'm grateful that the only one I follow is rooted in You. I choose to believe the Bible as the truth, and I choose to believe in Jesus and His words in John 14:6 (NIV): "I am the way and the truth and the life. No one comes to the Father except through me."

God, I pray for those who don't know You. Open their hearts to receive You as their one and only God. Amen.

THINK ABOUT IT:
How do you deal with conflicting religious philosophies?

I ACCEPT YOU, JUST AS YOU ARE

*If there is someone whose faith is weak, be kind and
receive him. Do not argue about what he thinks.*
ROMANS 14:1 NLV

Dear God, I don't want to be the type of Christian
who acts like they're better than others. So, I try to be
open-minded toward those who don't believe as I do.

Sometimes, when I'm with friends whose faith is
weak or who have no faith in You at all, I want to jump
right in and tell them why they should trust in You. But
then I remember Romans 14:1. There is a time to share
the good news about You and a time to remain silent.
I know, God, that You will tell me when the moment
is right. In the meantime, I will do my best to be an
example of Christ to everyone I'm with.

I live in a world of conflicting ideas, and I accept
that people have freedom to choose. I might not
agree with their choices, but still, I want to receive
each person with gentle kindness, like Jesus did. He
accepted people just as they were. Please lead me to
do that, too. Amen.

THINK ABOUT IT:
Do you find it difficult or easy to accept people just
as they are?

WHEN I AM AFRAID

When thou passest through the waters, I will be with thee; and through the rivers, they shall not overflow thee: when thou walkest through the fire, thou shalt not be burned; neither shall the flame kindle upon thee.

ISAIAH 43:2 KJV

Lord, there are times when I don't feel safe. Crime and violence are common these days, and I worry that sometime I will be a victim. I want to be on my guard and alert to my surroundings, but not to the point where it makes me afraid to live life joyfully—the way You want me to.

As a child, I relied on adults to protect me. But I'm not a child anymore! I am responsible for myself, and I trust You to take care of me. I will memorize Isaiah 43:2, and if ever I find myself in a dangerous situation, its words—Your words—will comfort me.

I believe, Father, that You love me. I trust that You are with me all the time and that nothing will happen to me without You knowing and working it out for Your glory. So, I surrender my worries to You, and wherever I am, I will not be afraid. Amen.

THINK ABOUT IT:

If you found yourself in a dangerous situation, what scripture verses would you rely on?

JOY!

*You will show me the way of life, granting me
the joy of your presence and the pleasures
of living with you forever.*
PSALM 16:11 NLT

Heavenly Father, have I told You lately how grateful I am? Graduation day is an important milestone in my life, and You've brought me here. I'm so happy, so joyful, to have reached this day, and I want You at the center of my celebration.

My heart is full, and You are the source of my pleasure. I'm leaving behind school, studying, assignments, and tests for a brand-new life. I can't wait to see what You have planned for me. I'm excited to move forward into adulthood and to experience new things. But, always, I want to do what is morally and ethically right according to You. I ask that You help me with that.

I will stay close to You and trust You to guide me, and I will continually find joy by being in Your presence all the days of my life. Thank You for everything You have done for me! Amen.

THINK ABOUT IT:
How specifically has God helped you reach your graduation day?

LOST

The way of the man who is right with God is smooth.
O Upright One, make the path straight of
those who are right with You.
ISAIAH 26:7 NLV

Oh, God, sometimes I feel as if I'm stuck in a maze—one of those huge, autumn corn mazes where it takes forever to meander from entrance to exit. I walk through life for a while making the correct turns, but then I hit a dead end. I backtrack, and still I am lost. That's how I feel right now. Lost. I don't know which way to go.

I could keep walking aimlessly, or I could stop and seek Your guidance. That is what I've decided to do, God. Here I am. Show me the way out of this tangled mess. Instead of left turns that lead to right turns that lead to dead ends, make the path ahead of me straight. Help me to see Your light at the end of the darkness. Keep me from making the same mistakes again and again.

I'm not very experienced yet at living life on my own, but I trust You to guide me and lead me to the place where I feel content. Amen.

THINK ABOUT IT:
Can you think of a situation where God led you out of a series of aimless turns and dead ends?

IF AT FIRST I DON'T SUCCEED. . .

"But you be strong. Do not lose strength of heart.
For you will be paid for your work."
2 CHRONICLES 15:7 NLV

Father, I know there will be times when my path isn't straight. I will encounter detours and maybe some dead ends. But I won't lose heart. I will continue to walk into the future with my head held high and with hope because I trust You to lead the way.

My faith is in You. I know that You will never leave me. If I stumble or fall, You will take my hand and pick me up. When I'm weary, You will provide me with strength. I believe that if at first I don't succeed, You will be my reason to try—and try again!

Father, You have set me on this path and instilled in me a dream for the future. I will follow that dream and serve You in all that I do. I'm sure that if I keep going and don't give up, You will reward me.

Thank You for guiding me and loving me. Amen.

THINK ABOUT IT:
Has there been a time when you wanted to give up but kept going and it worked out well?

I WANT IT NOW

But do not forget this one thing, dear friends:
With the Lord a day is like a thousand years,
and a thousand years are like a day.
2 PETER 3:8 NIV

Dear God, I have a problem with rushing into things without stopping to think. Now that graduation is over, I want to get on with the next phase of my life. When I get ahead of myself—No. I mean when I get ahead of *You!*—I sometimes make mistakes and end up in a mess.

I'm coming to You in prayer today asking for patience. Please, Father, help me to remember to stop and think before I leap into something. I need to learn to listen for Your voice and seek Your leadership. I want to follow You wherever You want me to go.

Patience is hard for me. I hate to wait. But I know, Father, that waiting patiently for You to lead me will set me on the right path.

I surrender my lack of patience to You. Take it. Turn it inside out. Provide me with the ability to wait with peace and serenity in my heart. Amen.

THINK ABOUT IT:

Do you tend to leap into something new, or do you first seek God's guidance?

A PRAYER IS LIKE A TWEET!

And never stop praying.
1 THESSALONIANS 5:17 CEV

God, until I got to know You better, I had the habit of praying one long prayer every night. But now I pray all the time. All day, I send short prayers to You, sometimes asking for Your help and often just thanking You.

I've been thinking that prayer, today, is a lot like social media where I can post a message, a tweet, with 140 characters or less. That's the sort of prayers I send to You throughout my day—short, little messages that keep me connected with You all the time.

I'm grateful for our ongoing communication. I never worry that You won't hear me, because we're always connected. Everywhere I go, whatever I'm doing, You receive my messages and send me Yours.

You transcend time! As ancient as You are, God, in this age of advanced technology You can still relate to me. You meet me right where I am, and I love that about You. Thank You, God! Amen.

THINK ABOUT IT:
Are you in the habit of praying little prayers throughout your day?

IS IT LOVE?

Promise me. . .never to awaken
love before it is ready.
SONG OF SOLOMON 8:4 CEV

Dear heavenly Father, love is confusing sometimes. It comes on strong, wanting all of me. But should I give in to it? That's a question I think most young adults ask. When is the right time to give all of myself to someone?

I've seen friends give in too soon. I know that love doesn't always last. Passion fades. I've known love to hurt and leave scars. But I believe that true love shouldn't do that! So, Father, how will I know when love is true? I don't want to give my love away until I'm sure that it's the right thing with the right person.

Please guide me. Help me to be discerning and patient, especially when I'm tempted to give in. Teach me about love. I'm willing to wait until You tell me that the time is right. I promise to trust You, God. Guide me. Amen.

THINK ABOUT IT:

When do you think it is right to give all of yourself to someone?

WHAT IS LOVE?

*Whoever does not love does not know
God, because God is love.*
1 JOHN 4:8 NCV

Almighty God, teach me to live my life loving others with Your kind of love. The Bible sets the example for me in 1 Corinthians 13:4–7 (NCV). It defines love the way You see it: "Love is patient and kind. Love is not jealous, it does not brag, and it is not proud. Love is not rude, is not selfish, and does not get upset with others. Love does not count up wrongs that have been done. Love takes no pleasure in evil but rejoices over the truth. Love patiently accepts all things. It always trusts, always hopes, and always endures."

I want to commit Your definition of love to memory and then practice it every day of my life.

Father, *You* are love. I want Your love to shine through me to everyone I meet. Help me to love unconditionally and unselfishly, always patiently and with forgiveness. Amen.

THINK ABOUT IT:
How does your own definition of love measure with God's definition in 1 Corinthians 13:4–7?

I WILL SERVE ONE MASTER

*"No one can serve two masters. Either you will
hate the one and love the other, or you will be
devoted to the one and despise the other.
You cannot serve both God and money."*
LUKE 16:13 NIV

Dear God, I'm eager to begin my career. I've waited a long time and worked hard to get here. Now, thanks to You, I'm about to realize a dream. I'm excited to get going. I want to be successful and to become a leader in this industry. I hope to earn a good salary and live a comfortable life.

But, Father, I don't want my ambition to surpass my need for You and my desire to serve You. You are my leader, my boss, my Master. I will do my best to serve You first in whatever I do.

Help me to always remain humble and to give You the credit for whatever I accomplish. Guide me to be the type of leader that everyone respects. Teach me to be firm yet compassionate, strong yet kind, and respectful yet unyielding when it comes to what I know is right.

I surrender to You, Father, this new opportunity. I am ready to follow You into my future. Amen.

THINK ABOUT IT:
What would you do if your boss asked you to do something you know God does not approve of?

DON'T WORRY ABOUT TOMORROW

*Don't worry about tomorrow. It will take care
of itself. You have enough to worry about today.*
MATTHEW 6:34 CEV

Heavenly Father, I'm a worrier. I allow what-ifs to cloud my thinking. I live in the future instead of in the moment.

This is graduation day! I want to savor every moment instead of worrying about tomorrow. Today is a good day, a day to celebrate. Still, I know that when people ask me what I plan to do next, feelings of worry and uncertainty will surface. I want to change that, Lord. I want to live for today and keep my thoughts in the present.

Help me to build up my faith. I trust You with tomorrow. I trust You with every day. So, please help me to keep my mind on that. I know that trusting You is key to getting rid of all this worry!

Thank You for today. Thank You for this graduation celebration. Lord, I surrender my tomorrow into Your loving and capable hands. Amen.

THINK ABOUT IT:
Where do your thoughts most often lead you: into the past, the present, or the future?

HOPE VS. APATHY

*But those who hope in the LORD will renew their
strength. They will soar on wings like eagles;
they will run and not grow weary,
they will walk and not be faint.*
ISAIAH 40:31 NIV

Dear God, sometimes I feel apathetic. Life gets so out of control that I shut down and just don't care about anything. I withdraw, play video games, listen to music, or just lie on my bed and think. It's not a good way to be, God. I know that. But how do I pull myself out of it?

This should be a happy time of transitioning into adulthood. But, instead, I feel lost and out of touch.

The Bible says that if I put my hope in You, then my strength will be renewed. My hope is in You, God! Lift me up out of this place and set me down into life again. I know that whatever problems I face, You will bring me through them.

Rather than running away, I will seek You, Lord. I believe with all my heart that You are with me. You are my hope now and forever. Amen.

THINK ABOUT IT:
If you find yourself feeling apathetic, what can you do to transform your indifference into hope?

I AM RESPONSIBLE

When we were children, we thought and reasoned
as children do. But when we grew up,
we quit our childish ways.
1 CORINTHIANS 13:11 CEV

Lord, I've just taken a big step into adulthood. Graduation means not only graduating from school but also graduating to a new lifestyle. I'm 100 percent responsible for myself now, and I want to start acting like it!

My friends and I have had lots of fun, and sometimes our fun was careless. I want to put that kind of fun behind me. When I was a kid, I didn't often focus on what was going on in the world. But now it's time for me to take notice and see what I can do to make the world a better place. Sometimes I was lazy. I can't be idle anymore. I want to work well and hard—for You, God.

Thank You for my childhood and all the happy times that it brought me. Lead me now into maturity, and bless me with joy in this new phase of life. Amen.

THINK ABOUT IT:
What is your definition of a responsible adult?

HANDLING STRESS

As pressure and stress bear down on me,
I find joy in your commands.
PSALM 119:143 NLT

Heavenly Father, this time just after graduation is stressful. It's difficult for me to relax and get thoughts about the future out of my head. Will You help me, please? I need to slow down and unwind, and I want to do it in a good way.

Drugs and alcohol are easy to get, and I see many young adults fall into the trap of relying on those things to relieve anxiety. I refuse to go down that path! I choose to calm down by finding joy in the daily gifts You give me—especially the gift of life.

Teach me to replace worry with a joyful heart. Guide me to creative and godly ways to ease the stress. Remind me that I can always rest in You by praying and meditating on scripture. Take away my troubles, Lord, and grant me peace of mind. In Jesus' name, I pray. Amen.

THINK ABOUT IT:
Can you name several positive ways to relieve stress?

LOVE THE UNLOVABLE

"I give you a new Law. You are to love each other.
You must love each other as I have loved you.
If you love each other, all men will
know you are My followers."
JOHN 13:34-35 NLV

Dear Lord, some people are difficult to love. I struggle with the idea of loving those who are so deep into sin that they have no room for You in their hearts. Still, You gave us a law—love each other.

As I go forward into life, I want to follow Your law. So, please, teach me how to love the most unlovable, especially those who cause needless pain and suffering to the innocent. Show me how to redefine my idea of love. I want to understand it from Your perspective.

I will do my best to love others by praying for them, Lord. No one is beyond redemption. You can soften even the hardest of hearts. I will pray that they turn from their sin and welcome You into their lives.

Instruct me in Your loving ways, and guide me to be an example of Your love to everyone—and, above all, to those who are difficult to love. Amen.

THINK ABOUT IT:
What are some ways to love people who are difficult to love?

PRAY THEM FORWARD

*I pray that Christ will live in your hearts by faith
and that your life will be strong in love and be built
on love. And I pray that you and all God's holy people
will have the power to understand the greatness
of Christ's love—how wide and how long and
how high and how deep that love is.*
EPHESIANS 3:17-18 NCV

Jesus, I want all my family members and friends to know how much You love them. It troubles me that some of them don't know You.

As I move forward in my life, I promise to pray *them* forward, too—forward toward You! I will pray for them using Paul's example in Ephesians 3:17-18.

Lord, here is my prayer:

You know how much I love my family and friends. I ask that You come into the hearts of all who are lost. Fill their hearts with Your love. Make Your love the foundation on which they build their faith. And make their faith strong. I ask You to lead them into the Bible and to enlighten them about God's power as they read His Word. Show them the greatness of God's love. And, Jesus, throughout their lives be their guide. If they stray, find them and bring them back to You.

Thank You, Jesus, for loving my family and friends. Amen.

THINK ABOUT IT:
Do you pray for family members and friends who don't know Jesus?

I CAN'T WAIT. . .

*"Now then, stand still and see this great thing the
LORD is about to do before your eyes!"*
1 SAMUEL 12:16 NIV

Oh, God. I can't wait to see what You have planned for
me. My new life is a blank slate ready to be filled by
You. Where will You take me?

I know in my heart that good things lie ahead for
me. You've planned the whole journey, and You will be
my guide. That idea excites me!

I believe that You have designed some adventures
along the way. Take me where I might not go if it weren't
with You. Open my eyes to the world as You see it. I'm
eager for experiences that are out of the ordinary and
beyond what I can imagine. My life is in Your capable
hands, God, and I won't be afraid. I'm sure we will face
mountains and valleys sometimes, but in those places,
I will learn the most.

What an amazing trip we are about to begin
together—a trip that will last a lifetime.

I'm ready, God. Let's go! Amen.

THINK ABOUT IT:
Are you eager for God to lead you where you might
not otherwise go?

AGE IS ON MY SIDE

You have been dressed in holiness from birth;
you have the freshness of a child.
PSALM 110:3 NCV

Dear God, sometimes I believe that I can't accomplish great things because I am young. But that's not true! Those much younger than I am have started successful businesses. Some have graduated college in their teens! They allowed nothing to get in the way of their successes, and that is how I want to be.

I have dreams, Father, to do big things. Not to bring honor to myself, but instead to help others. I want to discover the keys to unlock some of the world's mysteries, and I know that if I do my best and stay focused on You, I might realize some of my dreams.

Age is on my side, and so is my faith in You. So, bless me with confidence in this next chapter of my life. Don't let me fall into the trap of thinking that I'm not smart enough or good enough or old enough! Bless me with success, Father, in order to help others and for Your glory. Amen.

THINK ABOUT IT:
What do you dream of as your potential greatest accomplishment?

THE ULTIMATE PRIZE

And athletes cannot win the prize
unless they follow the rules.
2 TIMOTHY 2:5 NLT

Lord, I'm a competitor. I always strive to do my best, and I don't like when I don't win. That's both a blessing and an obstacle. A blessing because it motivates me to try harder. An obstacle because it leads me to focus on myself instead of on You and others.

It's easy to follow the rules of a game or a specific task. But it's not as easy to follow *Your* rules, God. I forget sometimes that everything I do is for You, and I forget that You want me to be gracious when I don't win, gracious not only on the outside but also inside my heart.

Competition is good, but the ultimate prize is knowing that I have done well in Your sight. That doesn't mean winning the game; it means putting You first in everything. If I win or lose in a way that brings attention to You and gives You glory, then I have won the prize.

Help me to be a good competitor, Lord, so that I may honor You. Amen.

THINK ABOUT IT:
What do you believe are the character traits of a good competitor?

FULL-TIME JOB

Jesus said to them, "My Father is always at his
work to this very day, and I too am working."
JOHN 5:17 NIV

Dear God, I'm about to start my first full-time job, and I have mixed feelings. I love the idea of making more money and being independent. But I'm not too happy about giving up some of my freedom. I guess that's part of becoming an adult.

Will You help me, please, to adjust to this new way of living?

I need to focus on You instead of on money and myself. I want to do a good job and set a Christ-like example. I hope to earn respect from my bosses and coworkers. If I'm tired or bored, I plan to try even harder and never forget that I am grateful to You for blessing me with the opportunity to work. You are always working in my life, God. The least I can do to repay You is to work diligently, gratefully, and without complaining. Help me to be a good worker for You. Amen.

THINK ABOUT IT:

What do you believe are the positives and negatives of full-time employment, and how can you turn the negatives into something positive?

THE CREATOR

*God saw all that He had made
and it was very good.*
GENESIS 1:31 NLV

Heavenly Father, I'm in awe of Your creativity! When I study the book of Genesis and read about You creating Earth, the sky, and the sea, I can't help but wonder if You had a plan or if You improvised some of it. I wonder because I'm a creative person, and I enjoy working spontaneously, just allowing my ideas to flow.

God, my prayer today is that You will continue to develop the special talents You have given me. As I go forward, I hope to use Your gifts in my work. Guide me to freely express myself creatively, to plan when necessary, and also to improvise well when I need to.

I am grateful that You made me to be a creator, like You, and I'm eager to see what we are going to create together in this new phase of my life. Thank You, Father, for all the wonderful things You've made to share with us! Amen.

THINK ABOUT IT:
What kind of creator are you? Do you work with a plan, or do you prefer to improvise?

ALONE TIME

And he withdrew himself into
the wilderness, and prayed.
LUKE 5:16 KJV

Lord Jesus, You know that I like my alone time. I'm the type of person who enjoys being around people for a while, but then I need my space. Solitude is where I find healing for whatever is bothering me. Alone time provides me with clarity of thought, and it boosts my inner strength.

The Bible says that You needed time alone, too, time to be with Your heavenly Father and pray. Even when huge crowds followed You, and Your disciples wanted Your attention, You found quiet places where You could be by Yourself.

I'm concerned that in this next phase of my life, it might be difficult for me to get enough time by myself. Jesus, when I'm in a new and unfamiliar setting, please lead me to my own space. Create places for me to go where I can unwind without interruptions and spend time alone with You. Amen.

THINK ABOUT IT:
Where do you go to be alone for a while to relax, think, and pray?

ZZZZZZ. . .

*I can lie down and sleep soundly
because you, L*ORD, *will keep me safe.*
PSALM 4:8 CEV

Heavenly Father, I haven't been sleeping well. Too many things were happening just before graduation—assignments due, final exams, and getting ready for the big day. All of that made sleep difficult. Afterward, the celebrations kept coming, and I didn't allow myself much time to slow down and rest. Now sleep escapes me because my head is filled with thoughts about the future.

I know I can't let these thoughts get in the way of my rest and getting back to a normal sleep schedule. So, God, will You calm my concerns and grant me restful sleep? I will close my eyes and let my thoughts drift toward You. Any questions or worries I have tonight can wait. Take them, Father, and hold them for me while I sleep. Keep them from intruding on my dreams. Help me to sleep through the night and wake up refreshed. Thank You, Lord! Amen.

THINK ABOUT IT:
Can you think of several comforting Bible verses that you can meditate on when you have trouble falling asleep?

AM I READY?

*We capture every thought
and make it give up and obey Christ.*
2 CORINTHIANS 10:5 NCV

Dear God, I'm overthinking everything! One minute I'm calm about stepping into the future. The next minute my head is filled with unanswered questions and worry. I wonder: Am I ready for this next big step in my life?

I wish that I could make time stop for a bit until I know that I'm ready. But, of course, that's not possible. I have to move on, now, to somewhere I'm not sure of. Am I mature enough to handle it? I think I am. But. . . maybe I'm not.

Father, I want to get rid of the uncertainty. My faith and trust are in You, so I have nothing to be unsure about. You will go ahead of me and be my guide.

I surrender my insecurity to You. I give You my childish thoughts and ask You to replace them with confidence. Instead of wondering if I am ready, I *know* that I'm ready! You've brought me this far, and You will see me through. Amen.

THINK ABOUT IT:
What do you know about yourself that makes you ready to face the future with confidence?

EAT, DRINK, AND BE HEALTHY

So if you eat or drink or whatever you do,
do everything to honor God.
1 CORINTHIANS 10:31 NLV

Father, I need to give more thought to my health. I've allowed myself to develop some bad habits. Too often, I grab snacks or fast food instead of sitting down to a good, healthy meal. I don't exercise regularly either. It's time for me to make some changes and live a healthier lifestyle.

You created my body. And what a complex and wonderful creation it is! You designed everything to work in a unique and purposeful way. You made my body one of a kind, a work of art—and then You entrusted its care to me. You don't ask much, only that I treat my body with respect, provide fuel for it through healthy eating, and keep it in good shape.

I'm on my own now with freedom to make my own choices. I choose to change my bad habits and get my body as healthy as it can be. Please lead me to use it, always, in ways that honor You. Amen.

THINK ABOUT IT:
Do you treat your body well, or do you need to make some improvements?

SELF-CONTROL

*Like a city whose walls are broken
through is a person who lacks self-control.*
PROVERBS 25:28 NIV

Dear God, I'm realizing that it's time for me to get serious about living more responsibly. There is such truth in Proverbs 25:28. When I don't control my wants, when I let down my guard and allow sin to overtake me, I feel broken into—like a part of me has been stolen. I don't want to feel that way anymore.

It's time to grow up! I can't be lazy about showing up on time. Being late demonstrates a lack of respect for others. I have to be smarter about how I spend my days. It's important that I create and stick to a schedule. I need to be wise about my money, to budget and save. By doing so, I will be prepared for financial emergencies in the future.

God, I'm letting go of my irresponsible ways. I ask that You change me. Make me into a self-disciplined person with strong "walls" that can't be broken. In Jesus' name, I pray. Amen.

THINK ABOUT IT:
On a scale of one to ten, how would you measure your self-control?

MORE. . .MORE. . .I WANT MORE!

It is better to see what you have than to want more.
Wanting more is useless—like chasing the wind.
ECCLESIASTES 6:9 NCV

Heavenly Father, I am so blessed! You opened my eyes today and made me see all that You do for me. You showed me that too often I am guilty of wanting more.

I have what I need, right here and right now. That has always been true. You meet my needs daily, hour by hour, minute by minute, second by second. I can always count on You. I might not know what I need, but *You* do. You protect me from wanting what might not be in my best interest. I trust Your decisions. You bless me with countless little surprises, things that bring me joy and make me smile. I know that You love me.

Forgive me, Father, for wanting more. . .more. . . more. You hear my prayers. You know the desires of my heart. In Your own time, You will decide what I need. Thank You for blessing me with everything I have! Amen.

THINK ABOUT IT:
Are you satisfied with what God has provided for you?

GETTING USED TO "NEW"

*You were taught, with regard to your former way
of life, to put off your old self...to be made new
in the attitude of your minds; and to put on
the new self, created to be like God in
true righteousness and holiness.*
EPHESIANS 4:22–24 NIV

Father God, I woke up the day after graduation and realized that everything had become new! You gave me a fresh start, an opportunity to leave my mistakes and old ways in the past. Thank You! I'm ready to reinvent myself by learning to become more like You.

Be my Teacher, Lord.

This new life will take some getting used to. Lead me and guide me along the way. Keep me from becoming afraid to walk the path You set before me. Give me a positive attitude, and help me to form good relationships. Show me how to be loving, caring, and forgiving. Remind me to watch my words and to always honor You with my actions. Make me strong in faith and especially strong against sin. Father, grow me into the kind of adult You want me to be, and let me serve You every day of my life. Amen.

THINK ABOUT IT:
What do you want to do with this new life God has given you?

LOOK BEFORE YOU LEAP!

*A large gift received at one time in a hurry
will not bring good in the end.*
PROVERBS 20:21 NLV

I'm getting way ahead of myself, Lord. Now that graduation is over, I'm impatient to settle into my new life. I'm busy making lists and plans, but today You've reminded me through Your Word, Proverbs 20:21, that I shouldn't be in such a big hurry and want too much too soon.

You know that I tend to jump right into things, and that isn't always good. I've learned the hard way that jumping right in can make a task more difficult than it needs to be; still, I've made that same mistake again and again.

I will commit Proverbs 20:21 to memory. Father, please remind me of it the next time I run ahead of where You want me. Teach me to be patient and, as the saying goes, to look before I leap!

Thank You for Your constant love and care. Together we'll go one step at a time. Amen.

THINK ABOUT IT:
Can you name a time when too much too soon got you into trouble?

RIGHT WHERE GOD WANTS ME

"From one man he made all the nations,
that they should inhabit the whole earth;
and he marked out their appointed times in
history and the boundaries of their lands."
ACTS 17:26 NIV

Dear God, I've been asking You to show me the way I should go. I ask often what You want me to do next. I pray expecting You to divulge Your plan for me. But You have been silent. I've wondered: Why isn't God speaking to me? Am I praying wrong or doing something to displease Him? But, finally, I've found peace with Your answer: You have me right where You want me!

I'm curious about what comes next, but I don't have to worry about it. It isn't crucial that I plead with You to tell me Your plan. I need just to be still and wait for You to act. You know exactly what's waiting for me in the future, and when the time is right, You will let me know.

I trust that You have good plans for me. But for now, God, I'm content to wait and enjoy life in the present. Amen.

THINK ABOUT IT:
Are you content while waiting for God to act?

MY COMMENCEMENT SPEECH

From a wise mind comes wise speech.
PROVERBS 16:23 NLT

Heavenly Father, if I were to give a commencement speech, it would be all about You. I would tell of Your power and greatness. Without You guiding us, we would be drowning in a sea of sin instead of walking across a stage to accept our diplomas.

I would tell everyone about Jesus and how You sent Him to save us and offer us the promise of eternal life in heaven. And I would remind them that Jesus is still with us today in Spirit, our best friend, the one who is leading us into the future.

Then, Father, I would thank You for Your gift of education, for the ability to learn and for teachers to guide us. I would thank You for the support of our families, friends, and others.

Yes, Lord, my commencement speech would be all about You.

I'm grateful to You for bringing me to this special day. I couldn't have done it without You—none of us could! Thank You, God. Amen.

THINK ABOUT IT:
Would you be comfortable making God the center of your commencement speech? Why or why not?

JUST YOU AND ME

I and my Father are one.
JOHN 10:30 KJV

Well, God, it's over. Graduation day has come and gone and so have the celebrations. The whirlwind of activity has given way to an eerie quiet.

It's just You and me now.

My friends have scattered, headed in new directions. Many of us have said good-bye. School is our common ground. The memories we made there might be what holds some of us together as lifelong friends. But I can't count on that.

I can count on You, though, God. You will always be my friend.

It's just You and me now, heading into the future, and I can't think of anyone I would rather have at my side. We're in this together forever!

I can hear Your voice in my heart. You are asking again if I'm ready to begin.

Yes, Lord, I am ready—a little bit afraid (I'm human, after all)—but I am ready to leave this place and get going. Amen.

THINK ABOUT IT:

What can you count on about God that is never going to change?

TEN YEARS FROM NOW. . .

Dear friends, now we are children of God,
and what we will be has not yet been made known.
1 JOHN 3:2 NIV

I can't help but wonder, God, where I will be ten years from now. How will I change in the decade following my graduation?

My hope is that I will have grown in wisdom and faith and that I will be more like Jesus in my attitudes and actions. I anticipate many new relationships, and I believe that I will learn from each of them about myself and also about forgiveness and love. In whatever job You set me in, I desire to work with respect for my bosses and coworkers, to be a holy example for them, and always to work as if I'm working for You.

Where will You take me, God? What adventures have You planned for me? What will You teach me? I suppose as my Teacher You will test me. I pray that I will be prepared and pass each test to honor You.

It's time. Let's start walking, Father. Show me which way to go. Amen.

THINK ABOUT IT:
How do you think your life will have changed ten years from now?

THE ROAD AHEAD

You will succeed in whatever you choose to do,
and light will shine on the road ahead of you.
JOB 22:28 NLT

Father, I can see it—the road You have set for me! I am ready to leave my old ways behind and begin this journey into my new life. My first few steps might be tentative, but with You leading the way, soon my steps will be firm and strong.

I believe that You are guiding me toward success. Your idea of success and mine might be different, so keep me going the right way. Lord, if a goal I set for myself is not in line with Your will, then take my desire away and replace it with passion for what You want me to do. I know this road will have detours and curves. I trust You to walk me through them. If I become discouraged, please remind me to keep following You.

Your light shines now on the road ahead of me. I see it! One foot in front of the other. Baby steps, Father. Here we go. Amen.

THINK ABOUT IT:
Can you see God's road ahead of you? Are you ready to start walking?

SCRIPTURE INDEX

IF YOU LIKED THIS BOOK, YOU'LL WANT TO TAKE A LOOK AT...

3-Minute Devotions for the Workplace

3-Minute Devotions for the Workplace includes more than 180 readings that address the real-life issues of employment—integrity, office politics, coworker relations, and more—that can be read in 3 minutes! Written primarily for the office worker, this devotional will encourage you to rely on God's underlying plan for your life.

Paperback / 978-1-68322-237-8 / $4.99